THE DON'T SWEAT GUIDE
TO YOUR NEW HOME

Other books by the editors of Don't Sweat Press

The Don't Sweat Affirmations

The Don't Sweat Guide for Couples

The Don't Sweat Guide for Graduates

The Don't Sweat Guide for Grandparents

The Don't Sweat Guide for Parents

The Don't Sweat Guide for Moms

The Don't Sweat Guide for Weddings

The Don't Sweat Guide to Golf

The Don't Sweat Stories

The Don't Sweat Guide to Travel

The Don't Sweat Guide to Weight Loss

The Don't Sweat Guide to Taxes

The Don't Sweat Guide for Dads

The Don't Sweat Guide to Retirement

The Don't Sweat Guide for Teachers

The Don't Sweat Guide for Newlyweds

The Don't Sweat Guide to Holidays

The Don't Sweat Guide to Keeping Your Home Clean

THE DON'T SWEAT GUIDE TO YOUR NEW HOME

Settling In and Getting the Most Out of Where You Live

By the Editors of Don't Sweat Press
Foreword by Richard Carlson, Ph.D.

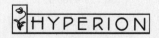
HYPERION

New York

Contents

Foreword

I once read a survey that spelled out ten of the most stressful things that a person could endure in any given year. On the same list (albeit lower on the list) as losing one's job, the death of a loved one, divorce, speaking to a huge audience, and other stressful things, was moving to a new home! In a way, this was surprising to me—and in another way, it was not.

On the one hand, moving to a new home is very exciting. It is, after all, "brand new," which can be a lot of fun. It's a fresh start, a new beginning.

On the other hand, we can't discount the stress involved in moving to a new house. After all, we are leaving our comfort zone, our friends, and many of our support systems. One of my sisters and her husband moved a few years ago with their four adorable children. They said that it was very difficult adjusting to new schools, new physicians, dentists, orthodontists, and all of the other important professionals that we sometimes take for granted when they are in our neighborhood. Even simple things like familiar restaurants, bike shops, drugstores, and department stores are very convenient, and we are accustomed to their convenience. In my sister's case, her family also had to get used to snow and closed roads in the winter.

In addition, many times, you never really know what a new neighborhood is going to be like until you actually get there. There may be unintended consequences, such as a child rebelling or a troubled or difficult new neighbor. There's an old saying: "Familiarity breeds contempt." There may be a grain of truth in this saying. However, the reverse is also true. Familiarity is very comforting, too. We know what to expect. Many of the variables are known.

The editors of Don't Sweat Press have done an excellent job at putting moving to a new home into perspective. They have provided a series of good suggestions that will help any move or transition happen more gracefully. I loaned this manuscript to a friend, who said, "They took the panic out of the move for me, and reminded me of the fun parts."

I don't know when Kris and I will next move from our current home. I do know, however, that when we do, I'll reread this book one more time. And each time a friend or colleague takes the plunge, I'll pass a copy on to him or her.

If you're in the process of or even considering moving to a new home, I urge you to read this book. A few good ideas will take you a long ways toward a more peaceful and rewarding experience.

Richard Carlson
Benicia, California, April 2003

THE DON'T SWEAT GUIDE
TO YOUR NEW HOME

1.

"Moving" Isn't a Dirty Word

Few experiences are guaranteed to strike as much fear in the hearts of grown men and women as the mere thought of a move. It's often said that moving ranks up there with the great stresses of life, including death and divorce! Upheaval is never easy to swallow, and moving can be fraught with practical and emotional difficulties. Leaving friends and family, changing your way of life—even just managing the details of a move can leave you feeling sad, anxious, and overwhelmed.

While it is difficult to escape feelings of ambivalence entirely, there are steps that you can take to make the moving process an easier one. A well-thought-out plan of action will help you get the many elements of your move under control. Each step that you take will build upon the previous one. As you get closer to the big day, your sense of pride and accomplishment will be strong. You might even find that moving provides you with opportunities for growth that you hadn't thought were possible.

For example, moving can be an opportunity to shed parts of your past that no longer serve you. Without the physical debris of worn-out, broken, or useless items, you can exert a conscious effort to welcome change. Celebrate the idea of making new friends, even while keeping in touch with old ones. If you're moving for a new career opportunity, enjoy the excitement that comes with setting new goals for yourself. Maybe you are moving to a new house or location that better suits your needs. Regardless, consciously embracing change can imbue your experience with positive energy.

When we shed the material possessions of a place, we often find that we are ready to move on to new endeavors. Do the same with your psyche. Rather than mourning what you are leaving, take pleasure in your memories, and look forward to making new ones.

2.

The First Step

Psychologists say that moving is one of the most stressful things that we have to face in the course of a lifetime. It's important, therefore, to embrace this experience, rather than face it with trepidation and anxiety. Moving can be a starting point for getting your life in order and your "ducks in a row."

Long before you call a professional mover, you'll need to go through your entire home and decide which possessions are making the journey with you. Many people take everything to the new location in a vain attempt to postpone the inevitable. "I'll sort through things when I get to the new house," they say. This is simply their way of avoiding the emotional pain that they fear as they are forced to make decisions about household goods, memorabilia, and all manner of personal possessions. The task that we fear is, ironically, the one that will empower us if we confront it head-on.

Our possessions are charged with emotional significance. That raggedy, out-of-style sweater that you can't part with, for example, may be linked in your mind with a happy time in your life when you enjoyed wearing it. Acknowledging our attachments can be hard work emotionally. It is the main reason that we long to transport everything and make those decisions later.

If you are moving across state lines, your mover will be required to stop at a weigh station. The sheer literal weight of all of those postponed decisions is now going to cost you—not only emotionally, but financially, as well. Take action. Begin the difficult process of moving with a well-thought-out plan. Each move is a unique experience and deserves individual care. Think of the suggestions in this book as a jumping-off point for your own needs and creativity.

3.

The Household Inventory

An inventory of your household goods is not only valuable when planning your move; it is an extremely useful tool with another practical application. You'll want to keep a copy of your inventory with your household insurance policy. Should an item be lost, damaged, or stolen, you will have a record of it. In the case of luxury items like artwork, expensive jewelry, and antiques, you will want to keep your certificate of authenticity and original purchase receipt in the same envelope. In the event that a claim must be made, you will have all pertinent documents in one convenient location.

Don't forget in this age of digital photos and video recordings that you can have a "visual inventory"! Your videotape can be kept with your papers while any digital images can be saved on a disc located in the same spot. For extra safety, the original photos can be stored on your hard drive. Having pictures of your furniture and fine goods will be useful if you plan on storing or selling any items that you own. Auction houses or consignment shops often require photographs for approval before they will accept merchandise.

This inventory will come in handy as you and your mover tally up what is being transported. Unpacking will also be easier, as you'll have a definitive list of what should have arrived. A little time and energy spent on inventory now will save you trouble and aggravation later on.

4.

Creating a Household Inventory

While preparing for your move, you may want to make use of a large binder. This way, all of the collected brochures, legal papers, and, of course, your inventory will be in one easy-to-access location. Be sure that you separate categories with tabs. For small, key items like contracts, you may also want to use sheet protectors. These are all items that you can find at your local office supply store.

"Inventory" is another way of saying that you are going to make a list. List the contents of each room on a separate piece of paper. It isn't necessary to count every pen, pencil, and staple in your home office. The simple designation "office supplies" will suffice. As you work your way through, you can place an asterisk next to items that you know or presume are not going to the new location.

If you have already found your new home, you can now make a list of its rooms. Allow each to have a separate piece of paper. Take a look at your current inventory. Does every room have its equivalent in the new location? The kitchen and the master bedroom certainly will, but are all of the items from each and every room going to the equivalent room in the new house? Very often, you will need to shift items and possessions. For example, for size reasons, the bed in your current guest room may have to be converted to a day bed and located in the home office of your new house. You want to be sure that you have this worked out before the movers arrive.

Once you create the master list, your inventory need only be updated with the purchase of new items or the elimination of older ones. Keeping track of this on a computer will make the process even easier.

5.

Dealing with the Mail

Like most people, most of your mail probably falls into the following broad categories: bills, financial communications, personal, and magazines and periodicals. The first step in seeing to your mail is to speak with your mail delivery person and find out when he or she feels it would be best to file a mail-forwarding card at your local post office. Contrary to popular belief, the change is not instantaneous. It can actually take up to two weeks after filing the card before mail begins to be sent to your new address. This lag time can cause you to miss important communications from friends and loved ones and put your bill payment schedule in jeopardy.

You'll want to write one generic "To Whom It May Concern" letter announcing your move to all your vendors. Under your return address on your letterhead (easy to create on the computer), you can type in the word "re:" and follow that with any account or other ID number that will allow the utility or business to easily locate your account. This one step will instantly personalize the letter.

Magazines and periodicals traditionally have some type of identification on their address labels. The easiest way to communicate with these institutions is to literally cut the address label off the most recent issue that you received, and tape it directly to the letter that you are sending regarding the change in address. Finally, any vendors that you don't regularly get bills from (perhaps your newspaper carrier only bills once a year) will require a phone call changing your address and/or canceling your account.

Make sure to do all this a few weeks before you move. It will help save you from dealing with last-minute minutiae.

6.

Important Change-of-Address Notifications

Losing the latest issue of your favorite magazine isn't critical to your well-being, but neglecting to notify the financial and legal institutions in your life can cause havoc. You'll want to be sure that these key players always have the latest contact information for you. In addition to sending them letters, you may want to follow up with a phone call to be sure that the information has been recorded.

This list will include: your banking institution(s), your attorney, credit card companies, all insurance policies (auto, home, medical), your stockbroker and any investment companies, all leased products, and any companies for whom you did freelance work during the year. (You'll want your W2's!)

If you are lucky enough to know your new location weeks in advance, see how many institutions have local branches near your new address. If you can continue with the same bank, gym, and/or brokerage, life will be easier for you. If this is not the case, try—either in person or by phone—to set up new accounts in advance of the move. It is critical to have checks from a local institution that show your name and address for local purchases. This single step will help you feel more welcome in your new neighborhood.

Do not forget your health-care providers. If you are moving to a distant location, be sure to inform your dentist and any doctors that you see. They may have personal referrals for the area to which you are moving. They will either give you your records to take with you or be put on alert that these records will soon need to be forwarded. You may also want to fill an extra prescription for any medication that you need so you have enough until the new health-care provider has been secured.

7.

Helping Kids Cope with a Move

If moving is difficult for the adults who have chosen to make the move, imagine what it does to very young children, who get caught up in the activity without any say in the matter. Fortunately, there are several simple things that you can do to help ease the time of transition.

Perhaps the most important contribution that you can make is to communicate clearly and often with all of the children in the household. Let them know not only that a move is about to take place, but also when it's going to happen, why it has been scheduled, and something special about the new home and location. In fact, if it isn't too far, take them to the new neighborhood. Point out one or two things that they can look forward to enjoying after the move. If the children are too young to appreciate these points, try to schedule diversions for them that will get them out of the house while you are preparing the move. This will enable you to focus on the packing and other tasks at hand.

If the children are older and involved in after-school activities like sports or music, be sure to research the availability of these activities in the new location. It will be helpful if your children know that the move doesn't mean they need to find new interests or lose the skills that they have developed. Remember that all of the positive lectures in the world won't help if your children see that you yourself are dreading the move.

Moving is a wonderful opportunity to teach children about the art of friendship. It may be more difficult to stay in touch when hundreds or even thousands of miles separate you from friends and family, but it can be done. In this day and age of instant communication via e-mail, it's even easier than it ever was! Encourage your kids to maintain their relationships with friends that they've left behind. Teach them that there are few things in this world more valuable than lifetime friends. Let them know that they will be able to share their new experiences with their old friends, and that it will add a whole new dimension to their relationships.

8.

Get the Kids Involved

Moving is a huge undertaking, both emotionally and physically, and should be a project shared by the entire family. Regular meetings are an especially effective way to discuss assignments and keep everyone abreast of progress being made. Try to schedule at least one meeting a week for the two months before the actual move takes place. The optimal time is during the dinner hour.

Family meetings are also the time to share feelings about the move. Young children tend to be frightened of the unknown, while teenagers may express anger. It's important to allow all of these feelings to be communicated in a safe environment. Perhaps you can share some of your own apprehensions. Here again, moving provides an opportunity for you to model behavior that will help your children in the future.

Almost all of us move during the course of a lifetime. This experience can provide practical know-how, especially for teenagers who may be going off soon to college. If you are weeding through your clothing and the household inventory, the older children can be responsible for going through their clothes and toys. The concept of helping the less fortunate by donating these items to a charity is a wonderful idea to instill in young minds. In fact, even the youngest child can be asked if he or she has stuffed animals to donate to help brighten a less fortunate child's day.

Teenagers in the home can help make runs to the store to gather supplies needed for the move. Packing their own unbreakable items like books, CDs, and bedding will give them a sense of control.

Children of any age can help you plan a farewell party to say goodbye to nearby family and friends. If you have photos and information about the new neighborhood, this is a great time to share it. Everyone will feel more connected to you if they can picture where you are going to be living.

9.

Preparing to Move Pets

It's just as important to communicate with the animals in your household as it is the children. Dogs and cats are especially sensitive to our emotions. It can be stressful to have boxes suddenly appear in the home. Animals may not understand an explanation about moving, but they will certainly understand an affectionate pat on the head and the feeling behind the words: "It's okay. Everything is fine."

If you are moving to a new state, you'll want to check the local ordinances before you arrive. You will have a specified amount of time to get a new pet license. Before you leave home, schedule a visit to your current vet's office. You'll want to have all vaccinations up to date and speak to your vet about your travel plans. Your vet will no doubt have specific suggestions how to make this easier on your animals. He or she may also have a colleague in the new neighborhood. Be sure to request a copy of your pet's medical records to take with you to show your new vet.

Animals are very comforted by clothing items with their owner's scent. If your animals will be confined to a traveling cage and out of your sight (for example, flying in the hold of a plane) be sure you tuck an old tee shirt in with them that has your scent on it, along with some pads for their comfort. You'll want to keep food, fresh water, treats, and toys handy no matter what means of transportation you use.

Once you arrive, secure a safe place to keep your animals while the movers are unloading the truck. Be sure to provide fresh food, toys, shade from the sun, warmth if it's cold outside, and someone in charge of bathroom breaks. You'll want to have fresh water available at all times. Don't forget to feed your animals as close as possible to their regular schedule. Remember that while you have elected to make this move, they have no idea what is taking place or why.

10.

Turning Utilities Off and On

The easiest moving scenario in terms of utilities is a move across town. You simply contact your utilities, and the changes happen in their offices. You'll want your gas, electric, and telephone services to be shut off the day after your move is scheduled. This way, if there is a snafu, you won't be completing your move by candlelight at day's end or making coffee over a campfire. It's best to have the utilities turned on in the new location one day before your actual arrival. This way, you'll be sure you have the basics covered the minute that you cross the threshold.

If you are moving to a new location, call the phone company and request a phone book well in advance. Ask that it be sent to your current address. The front of a phone book contains a lot of useful information. You can also ask your real estate agent for assistance locating the local utility companies. In a pinch, you can call the local chamber of commerce for information. You may have a deposit with one or more of your current service providers. Be sure to request a refund. By the same token, if you have opened a bank account in the new neighborhood, your new deposit can be made easily, and the new utility account can be set up with dispatch.

Remember to charge your cell phone the night before the move and keep your charger in your emergency kit. Should anything happen with your phone service, you will not lose communication with the outside world. Don't forget to ask your cell phone provider if it has service in the new area. You may not have to switch to a local carrier.

Find out who provides trash pickup in your new neighborhood. A move generates a lot of refuse, and you want to be sure you have an account opened before you arrive, as well as a clear understanding of the company's guidelines for pickup.

The most direct way to deal with all of these service providers is via phone. It's best if you write down the name of each representative who helps you for reference. You can keep this information in the moving binder that you created.

11.

A New Internet Provider

If you subscribe to an Internet provider like America Online and use dialup service only, your path is clear. You simply plug in your computer to a phone line, dial in the new area code, and choose from among a list of access numbers. You will instantly be ready to surf the information superhighway in your new home.

If, however, you run a small business out of your home or prefer the convenience, you may use either a DSL line or have a cable modem. You'll need to find out who provides these services in your new neighborhood. Then place calls to open an account and schedule a date for installation. Some providers may request a deposit, and your local checking account will once again prove invaluable.

This may be one of the most important calls that you make, and it should be scheduled well in advance of your actual move. These days, with our reliance on computers, you don't want to get stuck for days, or even weeks, without Internet service.

12.

Is a Storage Locker in Your Future?

You may find that you cannot take all of your possessions to the new location. Perhaps the new house is not as large, or perhaps you know that the move will be temporary and do not wish to transport all of your belongings. Renting space in a local storage facility may be necessary. Here are some things to watch for when you are looking for a unit.

You'll want to be sure that the facility is clean, secure, and located in a safe neighborhood. Is there someone on the premises twenty-four hours a day or just during business hours? Is the facility secure after hours if no guard is present?

Do the walls between the units extend to the ceiling, or is there an open area at the top? Could someone enter your unit from the adjacent one? Does management offer insurance, or will your homeowner's policy cover your belongings?

When you place your items in storage, try to do so in a logical fashion, keeping related items together. It is especially helpful to have a written record of the contents. If you number the boxes and have a master list of their contents, you can draw a diagram showing the location of each box. If you are storing a bookcase, you can make use of its shelves. You can also purchase fairly inexpensive shelving units that will give you levels of storage space.

Depending on the value and type of items being stored, you may want to use heavy-duty plastic containers with lids to store your belongings. In the event of a flood, your items will be secure. Using space in this way usually also makes it easier to maneuver in the unit and therefore find items quickly.

There are some things that you don't ever want to leave in storage. They would include legal documents; jewelry; furs; anything living, including plants; antiques; and old tax returns and records.

Many moving companies provide long-term storage. In some cases, their units are in clean, safe facilities that are only open to tenants by appointment. Here, the security factor is increased and may be of service to you if there is a high value to the items that you wish to store.

13.

The New Neighborhood via the Internet

If you are moving to a large city, a wealth of information about your new location awaits you on the World Wide Web. A great place to start is DigitalCity.com. A map of the United States will pop up. You then click on the city to which you are moving or the one closest to it. You will have instant access to all kinds of information, including updated weather reports, restaurant lists, personals, current events, nightlife, a movie guide, and available jobs. You'll also be able to research grocery stores, cleaners, and pharmacies. If your nearby chain isn't in the new location, you will have an early introduction to the one that will be servicing your family.

Another helpful site is MapQuest.com. At MapQuest, you can get driving directions to and from any destination. Let's say that you and your family love Chinese food. You decide to celebrate your first night in your new home by ordering takeout. You'd be able to find a restaurant near you at Digital City and get a direct driving route by going to MapQuest.

Finally, don't forget to make use of your favorite search engines. If your new city isn't big enough for Digital City, you'll find a wealth of information if you type its name into the search box at a site like Google or Yahoo. Most local chambers of commerce have web sites that will direct you to town programs, schools, public libraries, and local businesses. Often, search engines will find these sites for you. Entering the name of your town into a search engine may also bring up newspaper articles, legislative happenings, and information about town leaders. Researching and understanding your new surroundings can go a long way toward making you feel like part of a community.

14.

Would a Garage Sale Help?

One of the time-honored ways to offload those items that you do not wish to transport to a new residence is the garage sale. These sales pop up every weekend during warm-weather months. A garage sale can provide some extra cash and help defray the cost of any move. However, it does require a lot of work and careful planning to be successful. The first question you need to ask yourself is: "Do I enjoy garage sales?" If the answer is a resounding yes, the odds are that you have been to many and are quite possibly experienced at holding them. If the answer is no, you might do better to call a charity and enjoy the nice feeling of knowing that you're helping the less fortunate—as well as the tax benefits.

If you are still undecided, consider a few other key ingredients in your final decision. For example, do you live on a street that is heavily trafficked? Having a garage sale on a quiet street is inviting disaster. Are you moving during the warmer months when more potential customers are likely to be out and about? People need to know that you exist! People also like a variety of items to choose from. Will neighbors and friends be able to join you? In addition to bringing more items for sale, neighbors can provide extra people power.

Speaking of customers, you'll need to find additional ways to draw them in to your sale. Your local newspaper is a wonderful place to advertise. Don't forget the power of well-placed flyers, starting at least a week before the event.

If you are feeling positive about all aspects of a garage sale, you should probably go ahead and plan one. Be sure to enjoy it, as well. The key here is to release your emotional attachment to the items that you wish to sell. You aren't abandoning them. You are finding them new homes.

15.

Hosting a Garage Sale

When hosting a garage sale, the first place that you want to begin is in your neighborhood. Are there any ordinances against garage sales? You'll also want to check with your neighbors. Garage sales generate extra foot and automobile traffic. You don't want to leave the old neighborhood on a sour note.

Your safest bet is to plan to share the day with others who want to sell some items and who are willing to divide up responsibility for running the sale. To begin, you should agree on an advertising budget. Place your ads and create your flyers according to the constraints of the money allocated for this purpose.

Everyone should carefully mark the asking price of each item. Tags for this purpose are readily available at your local stationery supply store, along with scissors, tape, and poster board. Realistically, not everything will sell, so you'll need a contingency plan for these items. For example, will the leftovers go immediately to a charity? If so, will the institution pick up or will you be loading cars that evening for transport to a charity in the morning? It's a little overwhelming to figure this out at the end of the sale day.

You will want to use inexpensive folding tables for display. Make it easy for your customers to see and handle items. Be sure to have lots of singles on hand so that you can make change. You wouldn't want to lose a sale because you couldn't break a large bill. Decide if you are going to wrap any of the breakable items for your buyers. If so, have a stash of newspapers and tape on hand and perhaps a collection of grocery bags for your happy customers to tote away their "new" treasures.

You will probably get a lot of neighborhood traffic at your sale. Take advantage of this opportunity to say goodbye to neighbors and friendly acquaintances that you may not get the chance to contact in the future. Perhaps some of your neighbors baby-sat your children in a pinch or watched your home while you were away. Be sure to express your gratitude and wishes that you'll find neighbors like them in your new destination!

16.

Eliminate Trash and Flammable Items

There are some items that professional movers will not load on their trucks. You would be wise to avoid them, even if you are planning to execute your own move. The items on the "avoid" list include explosives; paints, thinners, oils, and varnishes; gasoline and oil; candles; aerosol cans; corrosives; potentially harmful liquids, such as bleach or nail polish remover; and firearms and ammunition. In the case of the last items, you will want to check with state and local authorities on the proper means of legally transferring these items across state lines. This has become especially important since the tragic events of September 11, 2001.

The other items on the list are best disposed of according to the guidelines set forth by local ordinances. Contact your local trash removal provider for specific guidelines. It is important that you allow enough time in advance of your move to plan for this. Some trash collectors will not pick up hazardous wastes. Many cities and towns allocate special days of the year for hazardous waste collection.

Homeowners may be required to bring their waste to a specific location on a specific day. If your trash collector cannot help you, call your town hall to get more information.

If your move is a short haul and you feel that you want these items on your truck, try to place them on the truck last so that they will come off first. This can be critical on a hot summer day. In any event, do not take potentially dangerous items in your own vehicle or on any form of public transportation.

17.

Preparing a Fact Sheet

Your computer is the easiest tool at your disposal for keeping track of the myriad number of miscellaneous details, phone numbers, and contacts that accrue during the course of preparing for a move. Break your contacts into categories, and have the various documents in one folder. You can add to your list as time goes by and keep a hard copy in your binder.

It's so tempting to jot information down on scraps of paper and adhesive notes. This is, however, a true prescription for disaster. In the absence of a computer, simply three-hole-punch some lined paper and put it in your binder. You can create your categories with tabs.

In one section, you'll want to keep a log of the various representatives who help you at all of the companies that you contact. In another, you will want to keep your travel itinerary. This will include any of the following that apply to your move: hotel reservations, train and/or flight numbers and departure times, and car rental information.

These lists will help you keep track of your contacts. Don't forget to make a contact sheet for those who need to reach you! Be sure to list all of the current and pertinent phone numbers that you have for everyone in the family. This will include cell phones, pager numbers, and maybe even e-mail addresses. With this information at hand, you will save valuable time. Just be sure that the movers don't pack your binder on moving day!

18.

Care Providers

Moving to a distant location means leaving behind your favorite doctors, chiropractor, acupuncturist, and even your dentist. Over the years, you have probably been to some specialists, as well. The best way to find replacements is to ask your current health-care providers if they know anyone personally who practices in your new neighborhood. If they do, ask them to make a phone call or write a letter of introduction for you.

In the absence of this kind of referral, ask any family members or friends living in your new neighborhood who they go to for care. If you are moving far away and have no personal contacts, try the obvious choices: your insurance carrier, the phone book, and even the chamber of commerce. It's certainly appropriate to interview your prospective health-care provider. After all, your relationship is hopefully going to be a long one. You don't want to make this important decision in a casual manner.

If possible, obtain copies of your records from your current health-care professionals in advance of your move. You can always have them sent to your new doctors after you've moved, but should an emergency arise before you've seen your new care providers, you'll want to be prepared. Set up your new medical contacts soon after your new arrival. If something does go wrong, you'll know there will be someone that you've decided to trust who is ready to help.

19.

Your New School System

To locate schools in your new neighborhood, you can check the Internet for your area or call the school district directly. If your children are to attend a public school, you'll want to find out what documents from their current school you'll need to furnish. You'll also need to know the process used to enroll new children in the school system.

Many parents feel that moving at the start or end of a school year is the best, but experience shows that children are far more adaptable than adults. Sometimes, the midyear move is actually easier on the child.

Private schools are another matter. Both of the information sources cited above will be able to direct you to the local private schools. Their requirements and fee structure may be quite different. No matter what type of school you prefer, you'll want to factor in items like commute time for the children, the public transportation available (commensurate with their ages), your ability to function as part of a parent carpool system, and, perhaps most critical of all, the ratings that the schools have for academic excellence.

If you are within driving distance from the schools in question, you may be able to arrange a tour of the campuses. This will no doubt influence your child's ultimate choice. If the new neighborhood is far away, be sure to request literature and photograph the campus when you are in the area to help finalize the house-hunting process.

Make a list of the pros and cons of each school, and call a family meeting to discuss these with your children. The more excited you can make them about courses and facilities, the easier the transition will be. It's also a key factor to make children feel that they have some input in the matter. Children will naturally feel anxious about moving to a new school. They may fear that they won't fit in or make new friends. Instill confidence in them with an upbeat attitude. If they see that you have faith in their abilities to navigate the social waters of a new environment, they will be surer of themselves. Listen closely to their words, empathize with their anxiety, and then reassure them. Change is a valuable and necessary part of life, and it usually serves us well in the years ahead.

20.

The Ins and Outs of the Neighborhood

If you are moving to a new neighborhood in the same city, spend a few hours scoping out the area, and then introduce the rest of your family on a weekend outing. If you are moving far away, you might want to check out restaurants, dry cleaners, supermarkets, banks, and beauty salons when you're in the area and tell your family about what you've found in the days leading up to the move.

Once you decide on a new home, you might want to seek out some of the places that will offer your children a continuation of their extracurricular interests. For example, for a teenager who rides horses, what could please her more than to receive a surprise photo in the mail of the stable closest to her new home?

Don't forget that many of the businesses that you deal with may have branches in the new area. Your bank, gym, and grocery store are likely candidates. If not, some of them may have special agreements with local entities that will enable you to transfer your memberships. Acquaint yourself with the local newspapers. This will provide a wealth of information, as well, on local and citywide sales and social happenings.

In the end, few things will acquaint you more with the intimate details of your new area than a few long walks. Whether in a home or apartment, introduce yourself to your neighbors. Find out, if they seem amenable to a conversation, where the local fire station is, how close the local police precinct is, and if there is a neighborhood watch that you might join. If you invest yourself in your new surroundings, you will turn your house into a home in no time.

21.

Finding a Spiritual Home

Perhaps you've moved from an area where you had been living for some time. You had roots in the community. You felt grounded and protected by the connections that you had made with neighbors, friends, and community members. You probably belonged to a spiritual center or house of worship, as well. The combination of these support systems enriched your life and sense of security. It defined what being a member of a community is for you.

If you find yourself feeling disconnected and lonely in your new location, there are ways to find a sense of belonging and community. Perhaps most importantly, you'll want to find a new house of worship for your family. If your particular denomination has several locations in the new neighborhood, you may want to sample services at all of them to see where you feel most welcome. Be sure to call in advance to find out what membership requirements must be met should your family decide to join.

Becoming active in a spiritual community can go a long way toward making you feel at home in unfamiliar surroundings. Larger houses of worship have official greeting committees designed to make new members not only feel welcome but become aware of all that the facility has to offer. Involving yourself in familiar rituals can help you deal with the often scary social scenario of making new friends. Being among people who share the same values and beliefs can ease any anxiety that you may have about feeling adrift in your new home. Practically speaking, people whose judgment you trust can offer you advice on schools, doctors, and community services.

If no such committee exists where you have chosen to worship, why not volunteer to start one? You'll automatically establish yourself as an ambassador to your community, and you will help your own needs for connection, friendship, and social interaction to be met.

22.

Vehicle Transfers

When you move to a new state, you will need to transfer your automobile registration and secure new license plates. If you are a member of any automobile association, that group should be able to guide you through the process. In fact, they may be able to handle many of the details.

If not, you will want to contact the Department of Motor Vehicles (DMV) in your new city as soon as you choose the new location. The paperwork involved can sometimes take time. You'll want to jump-start the process as early as possible because you will be granted a set amount of time to accomplish this transfer. In most large cities, the DMV will make specific appointments in advance. This can cut down on the time that you need to spend in the DMV waiting room. You many even be able to take care of the details over the Internet. Many DMVs now have web sites offering online forms and ways to process changes without ever setting foot in their offices.

Should your automobile be leased, you'll want to contact the dealership where you made your deal to find out where you can bring the car when the lease ends. Whether you own or lease, you'll want to contact the financial institution to whom you now make payments to be sure that they, too, know of the change in your status.

23.

Getting a New Driver's License

While you are at the DMV, be sure to make arrangements to get a local license. This usually involves taking a new photo, paying any local fees, and filling out the necessary forms. You'll want to check and see if you have to retake your written test. Rules of the road vary slightly from state to state, and your new home state will probably want you to learn the local ordinances. You can also check to be sure that you don't have to retake your behind-the-wheel exam.

If you have never driven before, but a vehicle is key to getting around your new city, you will want to request a driver's manual. You may want to take some driving lessons before you move. This way, taking the road test in your new home town will simply be a formality, rather than a daunting task that you need to add to your "to do" list.

If you are an adult learning to drive, it's possible that you will have some anxiety about taking your road test. As teens, we approach the event with impatience and great anticipation—it represents freedom and adulthood. Most kids never think about the consequences and real responsibilities which accompany being in charge of a vehicle.

Being aware of the great risks involved in even everyday driving may be what is causing you fear or worry. It is not wrong to be aware of the plausible dangers, but remember that millions of adults learn how to be safe drivers. It is probable that any nervousness you have about taking your road test will serve you well. You will be more likely to exercise caution and precision and will probably pass your test with flying colors!

24.

Gathering Personal Records

Most people know that somewhere in their homes or offices, they have pertinent legal documents. A move is the perfect time to go on a "search and recovery" mission that will enable you to have these important papers at your fingertips.

As you begin, be sure to clear out any personal vaults you may have at home. Portable ones will be making the journey with you, but they should be emptied anyway and then refilled and packed. Those that are built in to your old home are easy to forget. Another thing that is easy to forget about is the safety deposit box that you may have at your local banking institution.

The list of legal documents that you'll want to put your hands on easily includes birth certificates; passports; membership cards (gyms, country clubs, discount clubs); real estate transactions for the current and new home; school records for any children; driver's licenses; automobile registrations; prescriptions; and insurance policies (medical, home, automobile). You'll want to add to this list any documents that are specific to your family. For example, a family member with a long-term illness may have special documents that they need to have handy. If you are a nonresident of the United States, your visa is critical. If you cannot find any document on your list, be sure to call the issuing entity immediately to secure a replacement.

If you are part of a large family, these documents may fill an entire file box. You'll want to keep them in separate, well marked, easy-to-access holders. This information should travel with you at all times and never be entrusted to the movers. This is especially critical if the moving truck will be on the road for several days.

You may also want to pull out a few of the most frequently referenced documents and keep those in the moving binder that you created. Again, you'll want to create sections in the binder and keep some items in vinyl pockets. Small items can tumble out of a binder, and there will be items that you cannot hole-punch for legal reasons.

25.

Notifying Family and Friends

When you stay in the same vicinity, notifying family and friends of the new address and phone number can be done informally via e-mail, postcards, and/or telephone calls. After you get settled, it would be nice to plan a housewarming party to show off the new home. You might even impress a few friends or family members into service on moving day (or before) with the promise of a special dinner so that they can be introduced to the new place.

Of course, moving far from your current home presents emotional issues for those who love you. It's never easy to say farewell. However, in this day and age of instant communication via the Internet, no one ever needs to feel totally disconnected.

It will be up to you to make sure that your family and friends know this. If they are older, they may have seen relationships suffer once great distances separated them from loved ones. Assure them that in today's world this is not a given, it's a choice—and your choice is to stay connected.

You may want to send out formal notices of the impending move. You can purchase cards designed for this purpose, or with a user-friendly program, you can design them yourself on your computer.

If possible, plan a final get-together for family and friends before the packing begins. If a video camera is handy, have everyone record a message for you. Be sure to document the evening with photos. You can enclose snapshots from this event over the next year with birthday greetings and holiday cards.

By the way, be sure to have photos of the new home and your new neighborhood at your farewell party. It's never easy to say goodbye, so making your old friends familiar with your new life will provide a sense of closeness and proximity for both of you. Even if you can't see each other day to day, your old friends will have a sense of where you are and what you are doing.

Managing your sadness when leaving friends and family can be rough. It may help to remember that the memories you've made in your current location will be with you for a lifetime. There will be new and different moments to share with even your oldest friends in the months and years ahead. The changes in your circumstance can make for even richer, more fulfilling relationships as you and your loved ones explore new horizons and share new dreams and experiences. Even the saddest moments have silver linings—keep your eye on what's to come, and your friends will join you on the ride to the future, no matter where you are located.

26.

Leaving the Neighborhood

If you have been living in your current residence for a long time and have created happy memories over the years, you may want to create a special "memory book" as you leave. Take some photos of the house and the yard. Photograph family members and pets having fun in the home. Don't forget your neighbors and friends!

Just about everyone has a video camera or knows someone who does, so consider recording your memories on videotape. Include the children's schools, after-school activities, and other places in the neighborhood that you have enjoyed over the years.

Once you are settled in your new home, don't forget to share photos with the old friends and family members that you left behind. Let them see your new home, the kids' new school, the gym that you joined, your new house of worship, and perhaps a famed tourist attraction in your new city.

If there are older children or teenagers in the home who are having a particularly difficult period of adjustment, you might put them in charge of the "memory book." Kids today are very adept with computers and desktop publishing. Perhaps you can get your hands on a digital camera and let your teens produce a CD for you and your friends. They can include images, text, and music that highlight your fondest memories. Whether it's a photo album, video, or digital record, it will give kids a positive project to focus on instead of their sorrow.

27.

Preparing Household Items

If you are going to work with professional movers, you want to be able to tell them to pack everything they see. You don't want to complicate matters with a sea of "special instruction" items. In order to accomplish this, be sure that all items not making the trip are out of the house by moving day. Whether they are to be trashed, donated, or given to family and friends, handle these details as quickly as possible.

You may want special items to be packed by others. For example, you may want a local antiques dealer to come and pack your most valuable antiques. Be sure in this instance that they are insured either by your homeowner's policy, with a special rider to that policy, or by your mover's coverage. Keep the original purchase receipt and a current appraisal with your valuable records. Such items should also be taken care of by the time the movers arrive.

If you prepacked your nonbreakable items like books, linens, and papers, make sure that these boxes are sealed and clearly marked for transport. You don't want the movers asking you needless questions on moving day because you neglected to label some boxes. Time is always money, but especially for professional movers, who generally work by the hour. You will also want these items stacked and out of the walkways.

Other large items in the home, such as your rugs, drapes, special table linens, and comforters should be sent to the appropriate cleaners and packed for transport. Keep the rugs rolled for easy loading on the truck. The other household items like bedding and drapes can be kept on hangers for the move. The latter can be popped onto the bar in a wardrobe box.

If you are taking gardening equipment like a lawnmower or leaf blower, be sure to drain these items of gas and oil before they are loaded on the truck. Clear with your mover their transport of any liquid items from your garage (oil, paint, thinner) or cleaning supplies from the house. If you have multiple containers of an approved item, consolidate by filling one or two containers full. Then place these items in plastic bags with tightly sealed tops. Remember to do this with bathroom items, as well. Your nail polish remover, as an example, can destroy everything in the box in which it's packed if it springs a leak. Be sure to tighten all tops and lids.

28.

Making Travel Plans

If your moving truck will be on the road for several days, you will need to make special arrangements for your family. If you have any auto association membership, your dues may entitle you to free travel services. You can have flight, train, or bus reservations made for you.

The Auto Club also has excellent connections to hotels around the world. Don't forget to specify bed size, choose a smoking or nonsmoking room, and request a quiet location. You'll certainly want a good night's sleep! Be sure to ask if the hotel is undergoing any construction, and request a room as far away from the work zone as possible. Written confirmation will be sent to you. Be sure to keep these papers in a special section of your moving binder.

Once your moving dates are set, be sure to call the airlines and hotels. Booking in advance can sometimes yield a lower rate. With the high cost of moving, it will help to save wherever you can. Depending on the condition of your home, you may want to consider spending the night before the movers arrive in a motel or hotel. A lot can be said for the comfort of not having to make the beds or prepare a final meal.

Spending your final night in a hotel may also help you make the transition from your old home to your new digs. Leaving a place behind can trigger sadness and anxiety. By staying in a neutral place, you can take a moment to reflect on the past and look forward to the future in an environment in which you are not invested and prepare yourself for the changes ahead.

29.

Transporting the Family Car

Many people dislike long road trips and ship their vehicles to a new location via truck. This type of service is called an auto transport carrier. Your mover can put you in contact with some of the companies that specialize in this aspect of a move. They will give you specific guidelines for preparing the vehicle. You will have to arrange a pickup and delivery date as close to the actual move as possible. Remember that moving in winter in some areas of the country can be affected by adverse weather conditions over which your driver has no control.

Be sure to interview at least three auto transport carriers if you can, and work with the company whose representative you feel most comfortable with. As with your mover, check out the company's performance record with the Better Business Bureau. You should have a choice between door-to-door service and having your vehicle picked up at and transported to a terminal. Ask if the company provides insurance. Be sure to tell your personal auto insurance agent of your plans, and ask if your regular policy provides adequate coverage.

Another way to have your vehicle transported to the new location is to hire a professional driver to make the trip for you. Such a service can be found in the phone book, online, and in the classified section of your newspaper. Be sure to interview more than one service, and check the driving record of the person assigned to make the trip. Remember, too, that a family member or friend might be willing to do this for you in exchange for on-the-road expenses and a return flight. Be sure to check with your insurance agent before you finalize any plans for a third-party transfer.

If you are personally driving your car to your new home, be sure to have it serviced before you leave. You'll want to have a full tank of gas, an oil change, all fluids checked, and an overall look at the engine's performance. Be sure to tell your mechanic of any special road conditions that you may encounter en route. With your car serviced and your travel itinerary in hand, you'll be ready for the physical journey to your new home.

30.

Sharing Responsibilities

It's a rare move that excites everyone in the family. While everyone might not be "on board," there is still no reason one person should do all of the work. It is wise, however, for one person to assume responsibility for coordinating the myriad details involved. All members of the family unit can take an active role. In fact, becoming an active participant can help someone in emotional turmoil over the move channel his or her energies in a positive manner.

Break down your move into age-appropriate tasks that can be assigned to all members of the family. This is a rare opportunity for teenagers, especially, to assume adult responsibilities. Teens are usually in a hurry to grow up. This experience teaches them that being grown up involves more than just living without a curfew.

Here is a list of tasks or chores that can be given out at the weekly family meeting. You can amend this list according to your personal situation.

- Take care of all details concerning the family car: transfer of registration, transportation of vehicle, and so on.

- Arrange for safe transfer of family pets.

- Weed through possessions to contribute to the impending charity donation.

- Make travel arrangements for the family.

- Organize a garage sale.

- Make numerous fact-finding phone calls.

- Organize the farewell (potluck) supper.

- Create contact sheets for family, friends, and suppliers.

- Create moving day instructions for the movers.

- Notify family and friends.

Try to give each member a task that relates to his or her field of interests. For example, your teenage son's love of the computer may make him the perfect Internet researcher for the family's needs at the new location. Finally, be sure that family members have deadlines with their assignments. This way, you will stay on schedule.

31.

Working with a Real Estate Agent

Whether you wish to rent, lease, or buy a new home, condo, or apartment, a local real estate agent can save you time, money, and energy. Many people want to save the commission fee that they will have to pay an agent. However, you may want to weigh this amount of money against the benefits of working with a real estate professional. This person has the answers to many of the questions that you will be researching in the busy weeks ahead. A few key questions that a professional can help answer are: Which neighborhoods can you afford in the new city? What about the school district and its performance record? What is the tax structure for the new location? Are there any private schools in the vicinity? What are the best local business establishments for goods and services?

A real estate agent can help you find properties to examine that are not advertised to the public. Your agent will also work closely with a financial team that can facilitate your real estate transactions.

If you are buying a home, there are no added costs to you for engaging an agent. One of the advantages that you gain if you are selling your home is that your real estate agent will verify the buyer's qualifications on your behalf.

In fact, an agent can assist in selling your current home, as well. You can work together to establish an accurate selling price, prepare the home for showing, and facilitate the financial negotiations and transactions with the buyer and his representatives. If your move is in the same city, one agent can represent you in all aspects of your move.

In some cases, a large moving company, or perhaps the large corporation moving you to a new location, will be able to refer you to a relocation company that can handle many of the above details. A reliable, highly recommended real estate agent is, however, an invaluable member of your moving team.

32.

Hunting for a Place on Your Own

If your move is in the same city and you have the luxury of time, you may want to spend some days exploring new neighborhoods. Neighborhoods all seem to possess their own character. Some may be conducive to family life, while others may have a younger or more transient nature to them. Some areas are up and coming, and can be thought of as investments in the future, while others are tried and true locations that have remained valuable for years. Also, you may need to consider the proximity to your place of business, the quality of schools, public amenities, or convenience to public transportation. After your days of exploring have narrowed down your search to one or two desirable and affordable neighborhoods, you'll want to begin your campaign in earnest.

Ads for homes and apartments can be found in the newspaper and online. Don't forget to put the word out to family and friends who may be able to find out about a rental or sale that is about to hit the market. If you have a community bulletin board at work, post your housing needs. If you have some friends who work in real estate who will give you some insider tips, don't be shy about asking them for help.

If your quest is to rent, the process isn't that complicated. Remember that your credit report is going to be examined, so be sure to obtain a copy before you begin this process. You can call any of the three major credit agencies and request a copy of your credit history. This will enable you to clear up any discrepancies before you have to try to explain them to prospective landlords.

33.

Things That You Can't Live Without

The first consideration that you'll probably have about your new home will be financial. You'll want to create a workable budget and understand exactly what you can afford. The next considerations will be safety and the quality of the schools, if you have children.

These are key considerations, to be sure; however, don't forget the small things that make a house a home. Why not make a list now of the amenities that you cannot live without? Whether you have a real estate agent to work with or are doing this on your own, you'll want to be conscious of your needs. This is a personal issue and no two lists will be the same. Here is a sample list to help jumpstart the process.

- Is there a guest room with a bathroom attached?

- Is the garage big enough for two cars and the items that you'll need to store there?

- Does the kitchen have adequate working/storage space for your family?

- Is there a garbage disposal?

- Will the backyard be too much for your family to maintain?

- Is there a cellar or attic for storage?

- Is the house in move-in condition or will extensive repairs and/or remodeling have to be completed first?

You can make this list as long as you like. Standing in a home that you love, you may decide to forgo something you thought that you could not live without because the house offers other things that more than compensate. Just remember that you want this to be a decision, not a surprise!

34.

Getting Acquainted

Standing in a home that captures your imagination, you may be moved to make a decision about a purchase before you have factored in all the elements. Besides the importance of the amenities that a home offers you, there are also those amenities that your new neighborhood may or may not offer.

We all know areas in large cities, for example, that offer extraordinary homes for a reasonable price. Sometimes these prices reflect the fact that these grand old homes are near dangerous parts of town. Here again, working with a real estate agent can help keep you abreast of all the factors that you may want to consider.

Create a list of amenities that you want your neighborhood to have. Again, this is a personal matter, but the following can stimulate your creativity.

- If the city is subject to inclement weather, are stores walking distance from the house? If not, will you feel isolated? Is there adequate storage in the house for emergency food supplies?

- Is the neighborhood safe to walk in? This includes casual daily walks with your dog, as well as the walk that your children may have to take from the school bus stop.

- How far will the children have to travel to get to school? Does the district provide school buses, or will the children be on public transportation?

- How far is the house from your place of employment? Will you be forced to drive to work, or will you become a public transportation commuter? Are the necessary buses and trains nearby?

- How far away are places of amusement, like movie theaters, malls, and restaurants?

Keep your list with you when you are house-hunting. These considerations are especially important for those who are moving a great distance from where they currently reside. The new neighborhood is virgin territory, and you'll want to investigate until you know it and understand it like a local!

35.

Finding a New Job

Your first consideration in looking for a new job may be whether or not you wish to stay in the same field. If so, you'll want to start networking as early as possible within your profession. Does your company have satellite offices in the city that you'll be moving to? Could you, in fact, continue working for them on a freelance basis? Have any colleagues who now work for other companies in your field preceded you to the new location? Do they know of any openings?

Thinking along these lines, you can begin your quest with a list of calls, letters, and e-mails that you can personally generate to get the employment ball rolling. During this phase, don't overlook the wealth of contacts that your family members, friends, spouse's business partners, and any national organizations you may belong to can provide.

If you wish to change professions, your first step is to investigate exactly what is required to find employment in the new field. Do you have, for example, all of the necessary credentials? Will you need to take any classes or enroll in a degree program? You'll want to map out a practical plan of action so that you can convince prospective employers that you are ready to enter their work force.

A polished, up-to-date resume is in order. When you begin your mailing to appropriate contacts, this document will be your calling card and serve to open the lines of communication with prospective employers. If you are, for instance, making this move because a spouse has been transferred, and you are not sure what type of work you can do in the new city, pick up a book on resume writing at your local library. You'll learn how to craft a functional resume that delineates the responsibilities that you had in previous jobs, as well as the skills that you acquired, rather than a conventional resume that lists prior jobs related to your current field in chronological order.

Don't forget to register with employment agencies or headhunters in the new city. The fee that you pay will be more than offset by the time and effort that you'll save. It's also possible to register with agencies online before you move. Finally, don't forget to read the newspaper from your new city and get an idea of what kinds of jobs are being listed.

36.

The Best Time to Move

If you have the option and ability to move at any time, try to avoid the summer months. With children out of school and parents on vacation, this is a peak demand time for all moving companies. In summertime, you may not be able to get your requested date. If the move is a long haul, the delivery date may also be spread out over a week as the driver makes stops en route to you. If you can schedule your move anytime from early fall through the late spring, you'll probably have easy access to the specific days and times that you request.

No matter what month you choose, also try to avoid the first and the last few days of each month, as well as weekends. Those dates book rapidly. Again, you'll be avoiding the crowds with this strategy. Of course, these choices are guidelines for those who have total freedom of choice. Don't panic if you don't have this luxury. Moving during times that are more in demand is possible—it just means that you may have to put up with a few more little inconveniences.

37.

Finding the Right Mover

Hands down, the best mover to use is one who comes with a personal recommendation from a friend or family member. Lacking this, the large, established lines are your safest bet, especially for long hauls. You will want to call the companies and have representatives come and give you an estimate. Until you have your inventory, this step ought to be put on hold. Your mover's estimate is based on the weight of the items that you are transporting. If every room in your home contains a series of question marks when it comes to furniture, books, records, CDs, and DVDs, the moving company rep is going to find it impossible to write up an accurate estimate. With your inventory in hand, you will be ready.

This meeting with a field representative is your first experience with the company that may be carrying your personal property to its new location. Does the representative inspire confidence? You'll want to meet with at least three companies and compare their estimates and your reactions to their field representatives. Be sure to call your local Better Business Bureau to see if your potential mover has a high volume of complaints against it. This step will further help you narrow down your search.

One of your decisions during this meeting is who will be responsible for packing your household goods. A good rule of thumb that saves time and money is to divide your possessions into breakable and unbreakable items. Let the professional movers take care of the former (this would include glasses, dishes, antiques, and the like), while you place sturdy items like books, linens, and pillows into boxes. Your mover can supply all necessary packing materials, or you can shop at a box store.

Many people feel that in order to save money, they need to pack the entire contents of their home. Consider two things if you are inclined to take this route. Your mover is going to mark the boxes that you have packed as PBO (packed by owner) on the manifest that he creates on the day of the move. In the event of an insurance claim, it will be noted that items were probably broken or damaged because the professional movers did not pack them. This may affect the outcome of your claim and the value of the insurance coverage.

It's also wise to consider the drain on your physical and emotional well-being. Are you starting a job a few days after you arrive at the new location? Do you have several small children to care for without help? Will you have the stamina to pack the contents of your home, supervise the movers, and get the new house settled without compromising your other obligations? You'll want to factor all of these elements into your decision.

38.

Additional Services

If you work with one of the large moving companies, you will be able to avail yourself of additional services offered to their clients. For example, many of these companies are affiliated with relocation companies, or have a relocation specialist on their own staff. This person or company can assist you with details including community school information and names of local vendors. This will cut down on the amount of time that you spend doing research.

On the other hand, should a large corporation be transferring you to the new location, there will most likely be a relocation manager on its staff. This person can help you understand the company's policies regarding the transfer, including a clear explanation of those expenses which will be covered by the company and those which will be your personal responsibility. This representative can also help you understand which moving expenses will be tax deductible. In any case, be sure to check with your company's human resources department to see what assistance and information is available.

Finally, many large moving companies offer unpacking services, as well. Such a service may or may not be right for your family. It's important to understand it before you agree to add it to the original invoice. Movers will quite literally unpack you. They will cut down and remove the boxes and all packing materials. While this can be a lifesaver, you need to remember that movers are not professional organizers. In lieu of a sea of boxes, you will be left with a sea of unpacked household items. Whether or not this will be of service to you is a matter of personal taste.

39.

Understanding Your Estimate

It bears repeating that the key factor in receiving an accurate estimate is to indicate to your moving company representative every item to be moved in each room. Remember that the items and services added after your initial meeting will increase the price.

The most common estimate is based on the weight of the goods to be shipped. If the movers are doing any packing, the hourly cost of the manpower involved, as well as the cost of boxes and packing materials, will be added. Any special services will also be factored in at this time. Be sure that you understand how your mover creates the estimate. Some estimates are based on the amount of space that your household will take up in the van rather than weight. Local moves are very often based on truck rental and hourly wages for the employees.

If you are making an interstate move, once loaded, your truck will head to a weigh station. You are permitted to be there, so factor that into your travel time to the new location, should you wish to be present. If your estimate is a "non-binding" one, you will be required to pay no more than an additional ten percent at the time of delivery. You are allowed a thirty-day grace period to pay this difference.

If, on the other hand, you have been given a "binding estimate," you will be protected from extra fees. Be aware that you will probably pay a premium for such an estimate. Also, this type of estimate will be affected by any changes in the original manifest. In other words, you can't add large-ticket items like sofas or beds and not pay for their transport!

40.

Insuring Your Move

If a large corporation is moving you, confirm that it has an insurance policy in place to protect you. In addition, you'll want to discuss the move with your own insurance agent. You may be surprised to learn that your homeowner's policy will cover your belongings on the road. Give your agent your new address to ensure that you are covered on moving day. You don't want an accident to happen and find that you are not covered because you forgot to inform your agent.

Your mover will probably offer a variety of insurance policies. There is a basic policy, for instance, that provides minimal coverage. This is usually given free of charge. However, if you are moving valuable items and have no homeowner's policy and no corporate umbrella protecting you, this type of policy will probably not be adequate.

"Added value protection" will provide greater coverage. Loss and damage are paid, less depreciation. "Full value protection" provides for reimbursement for loss or damage based on current market value and is your best bet. Depreciation is not a factor. The higher the deductible you agree to, the lower the cost of the policy.

If you are transporting extremely valuable antiques, fine art, or collectibles, be sure that they are covered by a rider to your existing homeowner's policy and/or given special mention in any insurance coverage to which you agree with your mover. The mover needs to be aware of these items. Fine artwork, for instance, will need to be crated rather than placed in simple picture boxes. This extra cost must be factored into your estimate in order for it to be accurate.

Be sure to discuss with your mover the effect of the insurance coverage on items that you packed versus items that were professionally packed by their employees. Finally, the type of coverage agreed on should be written on the contract before you sign.

41.

Interim Storage

Large moving companies usually have storage facilities around the country. You'll be able to keep your household inventory safely protected until your new home is ready. This type of arrangement is often called for when escrow dates cannot be aligned or construction completion dates have changed.

Ask your mover if its storage facility is open to the public. In most cases, they are not. If you have to make an appointment to come to the facility, you instantly have increased protection over public storage, which in most cases is open to renters twenty-four hours a day. Private storage is a bit more expensive, but you will have greater peace of mind.

Keep in mind that storage, whether public or private, has a downside. Every time that your goods are moved, there is the chance of breakage, damage, or loss. In a normal move, everything goes on the truck at the current location and gets unloaded at the new home. With an interim stop at storage, your possessions will be unloaded and packed into the rented space, later put back on the truck, and still later be unloaded at the new home. Do factor the increased risk into your decision.

You'll also want to ensure that the truck that picks up your belongings is the one that will arrive at your new location. Sometimes, the load is taken to the warehouse and placed onto a different vehicle for transport. The truck driver is generally the owner of the rig and subcontracts out to the moving company. The driver making the cross-country drive to your new home may not be available on moving day and another driver and rig will pick up your load. You want to avoid this scenario to assure that those who originally loaded your things onto the moving truck are the same people who move you into your new home. You also want to be reassured that your inventory will not be moved on a truck to accommodate stops across the country that the driver has to make.

42.

Is Your Move Tax Deductible?

In general, a move is tax deductible if it is made for a specific job. If your current employer, for example, decides that you need to leave the Los Angeles office and move to Des Moines, you are in luck. Rather than guess, however, or take the chance of making an error on your taxes, there are several people you should consult when deciding which facets, if any, of your move are tax deductible.

The first call should be to the person who regularly prepares your taxes. He or she is in the best position to have up-to-the-minute changes in the tax law at hand. You will want to speak to this person early in the process, along with your financial planner, especially if a home purchase is indicated. You will want to factor in how much your current home will sell for, any changes in spending in the new location (for example, the change from public to private schools or vice versa), and the probable cost of the new home. Many of these expenses, in addition to your move, have tax ramifications. You might as well plan wisely rather than emotionally.

In addition, you may want to contact the human resources departments of your present and future employers (presuming they are different). Your employers may reimburse some of those tax-deductible expenses. Once you have your spending guidelines established, you should make a file for all of the tax-deductible moving expenses. You want to have those figures ready to compute when April 15 comes into view. Just for safety, you should also keep a file with all of the reimbursed and/or non-taxable expenses.

43.

Tax-Deductible Moving Expenses

The following list is meant as a general guideline. You can impress your CPA if you assure him or her that you will have all pertinent receipts from the move at your fingertips prior to April 15.

- Secure a list of all reimbursable expenses from your employer. Obtain any expense report forms that need to be submitted with the receipts.

- Keep all travel-related expense receipts (airline tickets, hotel bills, car rental and gas receipts, meals out).

- Be sure to keep all receipts related to the sale of your old home and the purchase of your new one.

- Keep all paperwork that you receive from the moving company.

If your move is a tax-deductible expenditure, you will want to keep the receipts for a certain number of years (determined by the person who prepares your taxes). The return is kept forever; the backup material (if you itemize) only needs to be kept a few years.

However, hold on to all expenses related to the purchase of your new home. These are useful in supporting the tax basis of your home. In addition, any repair or remodeling receipts will help you determine the selling price when the time comes to move to your next residence.

If you don't have a professional prepare your tax return, contact the Internal Revenue Service directly. The staff will be happy to send you the most up-to-date brochure outlining the specific moving expenses that are currently tax deductible.

44.

International Moves

On the chance that you are moving out of the country, you'll need to factor in some extra considerations. First of all, how will you be transporting your goods? If you're going to Canada or Mexico, you will be able to use a truck. If you are moving to Europe or Asia, for example, everything will have to be shipped across an ocean. You will most likely want to keep the bulk of your possessions in storage and start over in the new locale. Weigh the cost of furnishing a home from scratch against the cost of shipping everything on a boat.

If you call one of the large van lines in the United States, they can refer you to movers who specialize in international moves. In addition, if your company is sending you, the human resources department has no doubt transferred other employees and will be able to help you negotiate these unfamiliar waters. The staff will be able to assist you with information about housing, schools, medical and legal personnel, and local customs.

Be sure to call the consulate for the country that you are moving to and ask for a list of all legal papers that you will need to provide.

Consulate offices are located in most of the larger cities of the United States. Of course, you will need to start with a passport, and in many cases, a visa.

If you intend to travel with pets, be sure that you secure the correct papers and inoculations well in advance. Some countries have quarantine restrictions, and your pet may have to live away from you for several months. Consult with your vet, especially if a long flight is planned.

45.

The Bill of Lading

Every business has its jargon. While the term "bill of lading" may sound strange, it's really a simple document issued by professional movers. It serves two functions. First, it states the terms and conditions under which your goods are to be moved. Second, it serves as your receipt for the shipment. Be sure that your insurance agreement with the movers is clearly stated here. Also be sure that you understand it and agree with it before you sign it! Your signature indicates that your household goods have been loaded on the truck or van and have been released to the carrier.

Don't let the driver leave without handing you your copy. You'll want to keep the bill of lading in your moving receipt file. If your truck is going to be on the road for several days, make note of the number on the upper right hand corner of the bill of lading. You can use this number to keep track of the truck on the road. You'll find this same number on another key document: the order for service. Just as it sounds, this document authorizes the moving company to transport your household goods. You'll receive it after your initial meeting with the moving company rep once you hire the company.

One other moving document deserves special mention. Your driver will create a precise inventory of your household goods as they are prepared for transport. This inventory will note things like preexisting marks on furniture, broken items, and special items (like crated artwork), and it will also note the condition of any boxes that you packed. You will receive a copy. Each item will be numbered. As the truck is unloaded, it's wise to have the items checked off. If the truck has been on the road for several days and other loads have come and gone, this is an especially important step. This is a great task for an older teenager who wants to be involved with the moving process. You will be asked to sign the inventory once the truck is empty. Your signature means that you have received all of the goods that are listed.

46.

Paying for the Move

Be sure that your moving company rep communicates to you the exact method of payment that is acceptable. Let's say, for example, that you need to have a cashier's check and you forget to ask your rep how you must pay. The driver is only authorized to accept a cashier's check as payment. If you offer a personal check, your household goods will sit on the truck with the clock ticking until you either secure the agreed-upon method of payment or work something out with the home office. Needless to say, if this is a long-distance move and time zones are involved or if the move is made on a weekend, you have a prescription for disaster.

Some other common forms of payment accepted by moving companies are cash, traveler's checks, or money orders. Unless you are known to the mover or have made previous arrangements, don't count on using a personal check or a credit card.

47.

Filing a Claim

If you have done your homework and hired an established, highly recommended moving company with few, if any, complaints lodged against it, you will most likely not have a problem when it comes to filing a claim. Indeed, you probably won't ever have to take this step. Movers are human, however, and accidents do happen. First, you will want to examine your furniture and have all crated items uncrated (if possible) before the moving truck leaves your driveway. If something has been broken or scratched, ask the driver to note it on the inventory before he gives you your copy.

Try to unpack your boxes as quickly as possible. If there is any breakage or damage hidden there, you'll want to know as soon as possible so that you can quickly file a complete claim. Ask your driver for company policy in terms of any filing deadlines.

Within thirty days of your claim, you will receive acknowledgment from the moving company. They generally have 120 days to respond. Most claims are handled with dispatch. Your company may send a rep out to assess the damage in person. You can help this process by sending pictures with your original communication.

If your claim is not settled to your satisfaction, you can ask if your mover participates in a dispute resolution program. These programs have impartial mediators who will help negotiate your claim. For intrastate moves, you may also contact your public utilities commission for assistance. The Interstate Commerce Commission has jurisdiction over interstate moves. These agencies are not empowered to mediate claims. They can, however, determine if your mover violated any regulations in the processing of your claim.

Your last resort should be legal action. If the claim is small, you can go through small-claims court. For large claims, you will want to use a municipal court. In any event, be sure to let the Better Business Bureau and your local chamber of commerce know the resolution. People are often quick to share the news when claims are not settled to their satisfaction. Don't forget to give your mover a public pat on the back if your claim was settled quickly and efficiently.

48.

Preparing Electronic Equipment

Consumers tend to fall into one of two categories: those who have the original boxes and packing material for every piece of electronic equipment in the home and those who tossed that material after the ninety-day warranty expired. If you are in the first group, you'll want to either pack each piece of equipment yourself or have the box and packing materials next to the item for the movers to see.

However, if you live in an apartment with limited storage space, it is almost impossible to save all of the original boxes. Don't panic! Professional movers transport valuable electronic equipment all the time. They will provide the correct size boxes and necessary packing materials.

In any event, be sure as you unplug the equipment that you keep the necessary cables and wires bundled together. Ask your movers to keep all miscellaneous electronic components together in a clearly marked box. Be sure, too, that you indicate the correct destination for these boxes in the new location. In your new home, as you unpack, you will be able to hook everything up easily without going on a frantic scavenger hunt for the correct cables!

Unplug your computer and entertainment equipment the night before so that it has a few hours to cool down. This will help avoid the chance of a fire. Since computers are delicate machines, if you are traveling by car, you might want to keep the computer and your laptop with you. The monitor, scanner, printer, and other peripherals can be placed on the truck. Once you arrive at your new location, some technicians advise unpacking your computers and allowing them to acclimate to the temperature before you fire them up again.

49.

Fine Furnishings and Antiques

If you have a large collection of antique furniture and decorative pieces, you may want to consult the dealers with whom you regularly do business. They will no doubt have recommendations for movers who are used to handling high-end items. This is critical for their safe transport. Never assume that all professional movers are created equal.

Your qualified mover will help you decide on the safest way to transport your large items. In the case of extremely valuable furniture pieces, crating will most likely be recommended. While it is expensive, it does provide extra protection. In the case of small antiques, crystal, or fine china, experienced movers have the skill to safely wrap and box these items for transport.

If there are any scratches, breaks, or imperfections of any kind, your mover will bring them to your attention before each item is wrapped. The condition will either be noted on the package itself or the manifest. This protects you and the moving company in case of a claim.

If your collection is limited to one or two valuable pieces, you might want to consult with an antiques dealer. Have the dealer recommend someone who can pack your valuables before the movers arrive. Your dealer may actually perform this service. This is a good time to have an appraisal if you have not had one. It would be wise to photograph the items, as well. Consult with your insurance agent to be sure that these items are covered for your move. Remember, the insurance that your mover sells you will be affected by the "packed by owner" status of these boxes.

50.

Transporting Plants

If your move is local and you have just a few houseplants, it might be best if they were transported by hand. Your movers can certainly take your larger plants, especially the ones in outdoor pots, on the truck. The caveat here is that the move should be no more than 150 miles and/or be able to be completed within twenty-four hours from loading.

If the move is a long one of several days' duration, the movers will no doubt refuse to take any plants. It's unlikely that the plants would survive. It would be better to offer your plants to the new owners or tenants in your old place, give them to friends, or sell them at your garage sale. Don't forget that they might be welcome at a local nursing home, hospital, or school.

If you are bringing plants across state lines, check with your mover to be sure that there are no restrictions for the varieties in question. Whether transported by a mover or in your own vehicle across state lines, it's easiest if you take the time to obtain an inspection certificate. You can obtain one by contacting your state department of agriculture.

You will need to prove that your plants are pest free. A few weeks before the inspection, you might want to repot the plants into plastic containers—clay pots, while better for the plants, are more susceptible to breaking on the journey. If your plants are trailing varieties, ask your local nursery if it would be okay to prune them before the trip. In fact, your nursery is a great source of information for the specific needs of the plants you own.

Finally, if you are going to transport plants in your car, no matter the length of the trip, try not to let the foliage rest against the windows, as the leaves may scorch. Be sure to keep them propped up, too, so that they don't lose soil in transition or have branches break.

51.

Guiding Helpful Friends

As wonderful as it is for friends to help out, you need to have a plan of action and give them direction. As you know, there is no end to the myriad number of small details that go into successfully orchestrating a move. Before you leave your current residence, why not make up a list of phone calls that need to be made and ask a friend or two to handle those details? In fact, if you are all Internet users, your requests and responses can travel via e-mail.

In the final, often frantic, days before the truck arrives, ask friends to run errands for you. Have all items been retrieved from the cleaners and the shoemaker? Do you have books that need to be returned to the library? Are there any items that need to be brought back to department stores? Could a friend take your car in and wait while it is serviced? Thinking along these lines, you can make up a "to do" list that reflects your needs.

On the day of the move, if you're just going local, it's wonderful if young children can be taken to a friend's home to play or taken on a special outing. It's best if you stay at the house to answer movers' questions. Someone else can make a run to the local pizza shop to get lunch for the movers.

Once you arrive at the new location, depending on the size of the city and the neighborhood, you might want someone to stay with the truck until it is emptied. If the wardrobes (large boxes for hanging clothes) can be unpacked immediately, you won't be charged for them. Someone can be assigned to be sure that the house is set up to receive the movers. A bathroom should be designated for use by the movers and stocked with essentials like soap and paper towels. It's great to have coffee and muffins in the morning for everyone. Another useful task is to make the beds as soon as they are put together.

Make a wish list of things like these that you'd like to see handled by the end of the first day. You can then assign specific tasks to friends and family who have volunteered. Be sure to promise a special thank you!

52.

Specialty Movers

If you are doing your own move and you have a specialty item like a piano, grandfather clock, chandelier, or pool table, let the pros move it for you. Big-ticket items like these have unique handling requirements. You don't want to risk loss or damage.

You can find a specialty mover in the yellow pages, by calling your service representative (like your piano tuner), or by contacting the store where you made the purchase. A large moving company will probably refer you to the outside vendor that they use. They may also have qualified movers on staff who can assist you.

Consider a few of the key elements for each item. If your chandelier has crystals or other hanging parts, they need to be removed before moving day. You'll also want to have a qualified electrician disconnect it, along with any ceiling fans. If it's an outsize chandelier, it may require crating.

In the case of a piano, remember that upright pianos do not require any advance preparation. A grand piano, however, has parts that should be removed and packed. It can't be stressed enough that something like removing the legs of a grand piano should be done by skilled professionals. Finally, be sure to have a piano tuner come to the house soon after the move to check the instrument.

If you are moving a grandfather or grandmother clock, the weights and the pendulum will need to be removed. They should be wrapped and packed separately. Never leave these items inside the cabinet. Valuable clocks should be serviced before the move and again at the new location by a qualified clockmaker. He or she will synchronize the weights and the pendulum and level the clock.

Another item that requires special care is a pool table. You will need to have it taken apart by professionals and crated for the move. At the new location, a professional will have to uncrate the table, reassemble it, and level the playing surface.

One other complex item to move is a waterbed. Be sure to drain the water at least forty-eight hours before the movers arrive. You'll also want to take the frame apart and have the pieces ready for the movers to pack. If you have a problem with either of these tasks, you'll want to know in advance of moving day.

53.

Renting the Truck

If you are handling your own move, you will need help. You'll want to have a licensed driver with a credit card pick up the moving vehicle. Ask for help at the rental agency regarding the correct size truck. A general rule of thumb is as follows: The contents of two average rooms or less will fit into a cargo van. Two or three rooms will require a fifteen-foot truck; four to six rooms will find you renting an eighteen-foot truck; and seven to eight rooms will require a twenty-two-foot truck. Be sure to measure your big-ticket items like the sofa, refrigerator, big screen TV, china cabinet, bed, and dressers. Ask the rental company if your choice is going to be adequate.

You'll want not only the truck but also your load insured while in transit. Ask the rental company about their insurance rates. In addition, find out if your personal automobile and homeowner's insurance policies will cover you. Check with your credit card company, as well. You may have automatic protection that you aren't aware of or haven't needed in the past. This could save you a tidy sum. Find out, too, if there are any drop-off charges. Your nerves are likely to be frazzled by moving day, and you don't want any surprises, especially costly ones.

In addition to the truck, you will need supplies, including loading ramps, padding, straps, tape, a padlock, mattress covers, and dollies. The latter are particularly crucial and will save you time and physical energy. Make sure that you have adequate supplies for everyone assisting you on moving day. You don't want friends and family members standing around idle, waiting for the one dolly to return to the house.

Finally, make your reservation for your vehicle as early as possible, especially if you are moving during the busy season. Trite as it sounds, be sure to check the gas tank as you set out to be sure that it's full!

54.

Loading the Truck

It's best to appoint one person to be in charge on moving day. If several people are helping you, they need to know to whom they should address questions.

If you are leaving a rental, make sure that the owner or onsite manager knows of your plans. You'll no doubt need the elevator for long periods of time if you live up a few floors. Your "moving crew" may create extra traffic on the stairs. You'll want to schedule a walkthrough with the manager. Ask for a copy of the apartment inspection and damage report for your records. You may want to photograph the apartment before you leave. In the event of a dispute, this kind of documentation is irreplaceable. You may need it in case a part of your rental deposit is kept that you feel should be returned to you.

Before you load the truck, you'll need to decide if you are going directly to the new house or if one or two stops are going to be made. Have you promised someone your couch? Do you need to drop off items at storage? You'll want to plan if these stops should be made first or last and then load accordingly.

It is a good idea to have a second designated driver on the rental agreement. This can buy you more time in case the packing doesn't quite get finished. While one driver delivers promised goods and takes items to storage, a packing crew can be busy at home putting the finishing touches on the move.

Check your large furniture (sofas, dining tables, bookcases) for removable parts. Wrap furniture in pads and secure them with tape. If you run out of pads or none are available for rental, use household sheets and tape. In a pinch, you can also split large garbage bags and use them. Remember the measurements that you took and shared with the rental company? You'll want to use them before moving day to be sure that everything fits in your new home! If you need to take a door off its hinges or remove a window, you want to be prepared with the correct tools and gain necessary permission ahead of time.

Put the heaviest furniture for the final destination on first. Think of packing the truck as putting together a three-dimensional puzzle. Every piece must fit snugly. In a sudden stop in traffic, you don't want to hear everything shift, or worse, crash onto the floor of the truck.

55.

Packing Tips

Some budgets will not allow for professional movers. If this is the case for you, here are a few tips.

Unbreakable objects are easy to pack: books, linens, entertainment collections (CDs, DVDs, cassettes, videotapes), clothing items (shoes, purses, sweaters) and business papers, for example. Keep in mind that medium-size boxes are best. These items can be quite heavy and you don't want to injure yourself.

Don't mix items from different rooms in the same box. It will be incredibly confusing at your destination. If you have light clothing items in your dresser drawers, let them stay in the drawers for transport rather than using boxes.

Newspaper makes a wonderful liner for the bottoms of your boxes. However, you'll want to wrap individual items in plain paper made for moving purposes. Ink from the newspaper will make everything dirty, and you'll have a huge cleanup at the new location.

Wardrobes or "dress-packs," the big boxes that movers use to transport clothing, are practical but expensive. If your move is a short distance, you can leave your clothing on hangers and wrap it in plastic bags to keep it clean.

If you are transporting items that have been stored for safekeeping in the attic, basement, or garage (memorabilia, holiday ornaments), check the condition of your boxes. Very often, these boxes deteriorate over time without our noticing, and they will not survive a move. Invest in heavy-duty plastic containers. They stand the test of time.

Use several sheets of packing paper for each breakable item (dishes, glasses, pottery). Begin at a corner of the paper and fold the sides in as you roll away from you.

Be sure that your box contents are secure. When the boxes are moved, their contents should be buffered. Use peanuts, bubble wrap, extra paper, and the like to add padding.

Finally, if you can't afford a professional mover to orchestrate your entire move, ask a local moving company if it has any workers who "job in" during the busy season. You might be able to hire a skilled professional for a few hours and have him or her do just your breakables.

56.

Unloading the Truck

Make sure that you have a parking spot reserved for your truck in front of your new place. If you're moving to a large city, assign someone to stay with the truck for security reasons. Dollies are an invaluable aid on moving day. Their wheels, however, can damage your floors. Be sure to have some extra pads to put down on wood floors and carpeted areas. If you're out of pads, try some heavy brown paper.

The key to success in this phase of your move is having well-marked boxes. You'll want to have a few helping hands simultaneously bringing them in. What you want to avoid is explaining where each and every box is going.

While boxes are arriving, you can set up a command station in the home. The kitchen is the most common location. Your phone service should be turned on, but if there has been a snafu, be sure to have a fully charged cell phone handy. Remember to keep your crew well fed and provide a bathroom for their use.

On cold, snowy, or rainy days, you may want to have some space heaters on. The doors have to be kept open, but you and your crew can keep warm. Try to have some plastic sheeting available, as well. You can cover boxes as they make their way from truck to house. Remove the plastic once inside and avoid soaked boxes, damaged contents, and puddles on the new floors.

At the end of the day, be sure to gather all of the items that you rented for the day (pads, dollies, covers). You wouldn't want to be charged for these items. Your rental is probably for twenty-four hours. Decide if you want to return the truck that night or in the morning.

57.

Preparing for Professional Movers

The biggest difference between a moving day covered by family and friends and one orchestrated by your professional moving company is that on the big day, all delays will cost you more with the pros! Your goal is to be able to say one of two things: "If you see it, pack it," or, "If you see a box, load it on the truck." All of your decisions need to have been made by the time the truck rolls into the driveway.

It cannot be stressed enough that boxes need to be labeled for their destinations. A sign in each room designating the destination of all furniture and contents will help the movers. If you packed everything, be sure that your box labels are at once easy to see and easy to read. If your boxes and the furniture have separate destinations, be sure to make that clear in your note for the movers. The more information you can supply, the more time you give yourself to handle last-minute details.

Don't forget to reserve a parking spot for the movers. At a private residence, this is rarely an issue. In a large city, with hard-to-find parking, a little planning can help your driver. Instead of double-parking, for example, and perhaps having to move the truck periodically throughout the day, have one or two friends with cars take the spot that the truck needs until it arrives.

Be sure that your aisles are clear. Anyone not actively engaged in the moving process needs to have an assignment outside the home. This is a good time to check all of the last-minute details. Here are some examples.

Did you remember to empty all appliances and tools that have water, such as the steam iron and the wet vacuum? Your washer and refrigerator should not have been used for at least twenty-four hours. Ask your mover about the contents of the refrigerator. Depending on the length of the move, there may be items that he will not pack and transport. Make sure that the washer and dryer are empty.

To avoid confusion, keep items that you will be transporting yourself in a separate, well-marked location. Finally, be sure that items to go on the truck last have been grouped together and are so labeled.

58.

Helping Animals Cope

Your animals, like your children, take their emotional cues from you. Tell your pets frequently that everything is okay in a soothing voice. Give them reassuring pats on the head. Your animals are no doubt territorial and protective. If your dogs growl and bark at the movers, they are just doing their job. Don't tell them that they are bad or punish them—instead, praise them for a job well done and let them know that it's okay to stop. Your cats will probably fly to their favorite hiding place. To avoid all this upset, why not do one or more of the following?

Confine the animals to one room or area. Be sure that they have food, water, and toys. Check on them frequently. Be sure that your dogs get bathroom breaks and your cats have their litter box.

If your dogs have a kennel that they frequent, this might be a good day for them to spend being cared for and groomed by folks they know. Moving day, however, is not the time to give your dog his or her first kennel experience.

Once you arrive at the new home, introduce your pets to the house. If it's a local move, it would be wonderful if your dogs could go to the house before moving day. Show your dogs their new yard. Let your cats nestle in a room where they can be left undisturbed for a few days.

Animals will very often show us their level of anxiety by refusing to eat or go to the bathroom. Try to make the food more interesting, for example, by adding some gravy to the kibble. Take your dogs for a walk. They may not understand that their new home includes a backyard they can use. If the problem persists for more than a few days, call your veterinarian.

59.

Help from Older Children

Perhaps the best way to make your older children more comfortable in their new home is to give them responsibility on moving day. In fact, ask them before the big day arrives to think about how they would like to set up and decorate their new rooms. Allow them to unpack and settle their bedrooms. If they are old enough, make them responsible for breaking down their boxes and putting the packing paper in garbage bags.

Young teens may want to feel that they are valuable to the actual process on moving day. Perhaps they can set up the food for the movers and monitor the food area. Are there enough sodas out? Is there cream for the coffee? Have you run out of donuts?

Older teens can pack the car and help you put together those all-important emergency kits. They can also watch their very young siblings in the event that no one is available to take them on an outing. Newly licensed teens can drive to pick up the movers' lunch and run last-minute errands for you. No matter the age of your child, being involved in the process will do several things.

For example, sorrow and unresolved anger at having to leave the current home can be channeled into physical activities. Also, being involved in the process rather than relegation to being passive observers will raise their self-esteem. Finally, playing an active role in getting the new home settled will enable your children to bond with their new surroundings, making the new house into their new home more quickly.

When you're making a "to do" list for moving day and beyond, don't forget to involve your children, as well as your friends. It bears repeating—your children will be taking their emotional cues from you!

60.

Working with the Packing Crew

In most cases, your household goods will be packed one day and loaded onto the truck the next. If you have a small load, or if you have done a lot of the packing yourself, you might accomplish both phases of the move in one day. Your moving company representative will work this out with you.

Your crew will consist of women and men who pack for a living. It's best to provide them with working surfaces and then stay out of their way! They will bring with them all of the supplies that they need. You should make yourself available for any questions they may have. Again, it's helpful to have notes tacked up in each room with special instructions. If you are in the bathroom, with a young child, or called away for some emergency, the process can continue.

Have the family fed before the movers arrive. Wash, dry, and pack your dishes. Don't forget the dishes in the dishwasher! If you have items that need to be unscrewed from fixtures, do so before the packers arrive. Examples include can openers, drapery rods, and towel bars. Any mirrors or artwork that are hanging on the walls can remain in place. Finally, strip your beds, but let the movers take the beds apart.

No matter how much you want this move to happen, watching your possessions disappear into boxes is difficult. Be sure while making yourself available that you have practical work to do that moves the process along. Are there any final telephone calls to be made? Do you have any personal thank-you notes to write?

If the move is to take place the next morning, consider spending the night at a hotel or with family and friends. This way, everything can be packed, and you'll have a chance to rest and fully recharge your spirits for the long day or days that follow.

61.

Transporting Valuables

If you have valuable jewelry, furs, stock certificates, coin collections, and the like, your mover will not want to take them. Nor do you want to entrust your valuables to strangers. It's best to pack everything carefully and transport it all by hand. A trip by car is the logical choice. If you must travel by air, keep the items with you in your carry-on bag. Be sure that you have detailed photographs of your jewelry, in addition to purchase receipts and appraisals. In the event of a theft, you could have your treasures duplicated.

Should you have a large collection of big-ticket items, be sure that your insurance rider covers you in transit and at the new residence. Make arrangements for permanent storage before you arrive. For example, you may want to rent a safety deposit box in the vault of a local bank for your jewelry and valuable papers—or you may want to have a safe ready at your new location.

Make your plans for all of these items well in advance of moving day. When the movers arrive, be sure that your valuables are in a secure and separate location, like the trunk of your car, or suitcases clearly marked: "Do Not Pack." Movers will presume that everything is going unless you specifically tell them otherwise. You don't want to make a mistake with your most precious possessions.

62.

Creating Emergency Kits

Every family's emergency kit for moving will be slightly different. You need to consider the number of people moving, the distance, and also their ages. For example, in the sample list below, any supplies for babies and toddlers have not been included. If you have little children, you will have to make a separate list of diapers, changes of clothes, and formula needed for the time you are on the road, as well as the first days living out of boxes. By the same token, an elderly relative may have an extensive list of daily medications or even key equipment that must be kept on hand. You'll have to take your particular circumstances into consideration when you create your list. Here is a general sample to help you get started.

Personal Aids
- Toiletries
- Change of clothes

- Medications
- Eyeglasses/contact lenses and supplies
- Aspirin, cold medicines, and first-aid kit
- Alarm clock
- Cell phone and charger

Household Items
- Small tool box
- Lightbulbs
- Flashlights
- Trash bags
- Extension cords and batteries
- Basic cleaning supplies
- Work gloves
- Paper towels, toilet paper, and soap

Move-Related Supplies
- Box cutters
- Tape and dispensers
- Scissors
- Work gloves

House-to-Home Supplies

- Bedding and towels
- Paper plates, cups, napkins, and plastic utensils
- Coffee maker, powdered creamer, and sweetener
- Snacks
- Water
- Pet supplies

You may not want to use some of these items. As noted, your child care needs may be extensive. Preparing for move-in day and the first twenty-four hours after the truck leaves is a little like planning a trip. Your life in the latter instance gets reduced to a suitcase. Here, your key items must fit into a few boxes to be loaded last and unloaded first.

63.

Caring for Your Moving Crew

Moving crews become the most important people in your lives for about twenty-four to forty-eight hours. They handle your most precious possessions. It really pays to take good care of them! The following is a summary of points to cover regarding your crew. Follow them and, no matter what happens on moving day, your crew will bend over backward to help you.

- Have coffee and donuts waiting for the crew when they arrive.

- Keep sodas and water available throughout the day. If it's cold, offer to make more coffee and tea throughout the day. If it's a blistering hot day, have pitchers of lemonade out.

- Lunch doesn't have to be a feast. Movers will appreciate pizza or sandwiches.

- Your supermarket probably has inexpensive coffee cake or cookies. Have these out in the afternoon for the three o'clock slump.

- Designate a bathroom for the movers to use and keep it well stocked.

These small steps reap great rewards. Your movers will take extra care with your most precious items because you have been so gracious with them.

64.

Moving Day Meals

The easiest way to handle meals for your family is to eat what the movers are being served. If, however, someone in the family is on a special diet or you have babies or toddlers to feed, you'll want to plan some meals in advance. If you are moving a long distance and must defrost and unplug the refrigerator, place your special meals in a cooler the day before the movers arrive.

Try to eat out as a family at the end of your packing and moving days, especially if you decide to sleep at home. When you are expending huge amounts of physical and emotional energy, it's really crucial that you replenish yourself. One of the most nurturing experiences we can have at this time is a hot bath and a delicious dinner. Just remember: When all else fails, there's always takeout!

65.

Last-Minute Details

Let's face it: There's a good chance that Murphy's Law will come into play during the time of your move. No matter how well organized you are, something will not go as planned. Hopefully, it will be a tiny glitch in the process. If you are prepared for the misstep, you'll recover faster and move on. Human beings drop things. They forget to process orders made weeks ago. The weather can bring you unexpected hassles. The list goes on. A sense of humor will carry you through this time.

Your best defense is to get enough sleep and eat healthy food at every meal. Don't fuel your body with candy bars and tons of coffee to compensate for skipped meals. This isn't the time to go on a fad diet. In your arsenal of family and friends, you probably have one person who is unflappable in a crisis. Ask that person to be with you on packing day and the day that your things are loaded for transport. Let the person assist you in any way that's appropriate. It's okay to ask for help. Remember that you'll want to have the emotional and physical energy to enjoy your new home right from the start.

In the final analysis, the things that you are bringing with you to your new home are only "stuff." The health and safety of your family are what matter most.

66.

The New Owners

If you are renting a home or apartment, you'll want to leave the space in good condition in order to get your security deposit back in a timely fashion. If you are leaving a home that you own, gather the warranties and instruction booklets for all appliances and leave them in a prominent place.

You'll want to do a final walkthrough after the truck leaves. Did you take the garbage out of every room? Was everything removed from all closets, the attic, crawlspaces, and garage? If you have a built-in home safe, did you remember to empty it? Have all of your possessions been removed from the front and backyards? Children and dogs have a remarkable ability to lose toys in bushes. Be sure that you check every nook and cranny!

You don't have to clean the house from top to bottom, but you do want to leave it in a presentable fashion. After all, isn't that what you hope to find at your new location? Turn off the water heater, and leave the thermostat at fifty-five degrees. Leave the new owners your forwarding address on the off chance that the postal system lets a few pieces of mail slip through the cracks.

Take your telephones with you as you exit, unless they are part of the purchase agreement. Be sure as you exit for the last time that the oven is turned off. Create a place to hide house keys, and be sure to communicate that place in advance.

If you are organized on packing and moving days and find yourself with some free time, you might want to leave the new owners a "cheat sheet" about the neighborhood. You can list the plumbers, electricians, sanitation company, and others who service the house. This kind of note is indeed above and beyond the call of duty. It is, however, a very civilized touch. Who knows? You might find the same treat waiting at your new home!

67.

Saving with Boxes

If you are engaging professional movers to pack for you, they will supply their own boxes and packing materials. If you have help settling in at the new location, you'll want to unpack and remove as many boxes as you can while the moving truck is in the driveway. Your movers will take those boxes for you. You won't even have to cut them down.

You'll discover that lots of large boxes hold only one item. The classic example is the box used to pack a lampshade. If you have four or five lampshades and you unpack them immediately, that's four or five large boxes out of your new home. You'll not only have more space, you won't have to cut down the boxes and arrange for trash pickup.

If you are packing for yourself and don't have the money to purchase all new boxes (you will, however, want new boxes for items like clothing and linens), there are two places to find sturdy boxes for free. Your supermarket or liquor store will have boxes that transported liquid products like alcohol and detergent. These are reinforced boxes in reasonable sizes that will be great for things like books and toys.

Your other source is moving trucks—scour your neighborhood for them on weekends. Arrange to pick up the empty boxes from someone else's move. No doubt, the new resident will be grateful. With any luck, someone in your new city will have a similar need!

68.

Is Tipping Customary?

The sad truth is that professional movers rarely receive tips. If your movers do a sloppy job, they certainly don't deserve to be rewarded. Movers are not, however, unlike waiters in a good restaurant: You are paying a premium for the food, but a good tip is expected if the service has been professional and to your liking. You wouldn't say, for instance, "I paid so much for this food, I have no intention of leaving a tip!" Yet that's exactly what most people say about tipping a mover. "I paid such a high price for this move, a tip is not necessary."

Your fee includes packing materials, hourly wages, and truck rental. The men and women entrusted with the task of packing and transporting your possessions truly have a part of you in their hands. If you like the way they fulfill their duties, a tip is always appreciated. You can reward the individual movers, or you can give the money to the driver or supervisor and ask that he or she distribute the funds.

If you do decide to reward your movers, have cash on hand. Extra monies added to the check or credit card payment (if this form of payment has been approved) may not make their way back to the movers' hands. Very often, these sums are paid to the company.

69.

Tracking Your Move

If your move is local, you might want to follow the truck to be sure that you arrive at the new location at the same time. You can certainly exchange cell phone numbers with the driver in case you get separated in traffic. In the best-case scenario, you can have someone at the new house, setting it up for the movers while you are helping them get the truck loaded. Short moves do not pose a serious need to track your truck.

On longer moves, as noted earlier, you'll want to use the number on your bill of lading as your tracking number to contact your moving company and find out the current status of your load. Your moving company should have a twenty-four-hour fix on your truck.

Trucks taking multiple loads across the country often make many stops. They want to keep the truck full at all times, as that is more profitable. If you establish a good rapport with your driver on moving day, you can trade cell phone numbers. Then you'll be getting your updates straight from the horse's mouth.

70.

Children and Animals in Transit

Let's be honest. The most organized move leaves one physically, emotionally, and mentally exhausted. Young children who don't quite understand what is happening and older children who aren't exactly thrilled about the process are going to complicate the mix. The best way to survive is to have activities to keep every age group occupied. You don't want endless hours of "Are we there yet?"

If you have a vehicle, be sure to stock it with best-loved toys for the younger children. Bring activities like coloring books and books to read. Don't forget that favorite doll or stuffed animal. You'll want the kids to be able to amuse themselves as much as possible.

Bring CD players and electronic games for your older children and teens. They will more than likely be delighted to tune out their surroundings and go into their own world. If you are renting a vehicle, there are large vans and SUVs that have DVD or video players installed. These will surely occupy all of your travelers!

Of course, your four-legged travelers won't care about any of these amenities, so other arrangements must be made. Your animals are in many ways like your very young children. They will be comforted to be with you but deeply confused and needy. They will want their favorite toys for a sense of security. Stop at regular intervals so that your dogs can relieve themselves and get a drink, as well. Carry everyone's favorite treats to snack on, no matter how many legs they have! When it comes to regular meals in transit, be sure to speak to your vet. Some animals travel better on an empty stomach. Be sure that any animals traveling in cages have adequate water.

Finally, if your dogs or cats are not used to traveling by car, they are apt to develop motion sickness. Enjoying car travel is an acquired ability for most animals. If you can, take your pets for short trips in the car for several weeks before the move. They will have a chance to get their bodies acclimated to travel. The last thing that you need is to have to stop and clean up after Fido heaves his breakfast in the rental.

71.

Preparing Your Home for Sale

If you want your house to sell quickly, you want to price it realistically, and you want to show off its best features to prospective buyers. Is there a remodeling job that you have been putting off? Now may be the time to do some of those upgrades that you know will add value to the home. Don't forget the outside! Does your home need a good paint job? Is the landscape dull and lackluster? Are your windows clean? Remember the old adage, "You don't have a second chance to make a first impression." Neither does your home.

As you create your inventory and prepare to clear out items that are either going to charity or are to be permanently "retired," you will also be readying your home for a quick sale. Crowded rooms, jammed closets, piles of old magazines, wayward toys scattered all over the floor, and unopened mail make a home feel cramped and unwelcoming.

Your preparations for your move will have the added benefit of helping to make your current home ready for viewing. After all, in the best of all possible worlds, you want your current home to sell before you leave for your new one.

Once you feel that the house is reasonably free of clutter and extraneous pieces of furniture, walk outside and reenter your home as if for the first time. If you were a prospective buyer, what would grab your attention, both negatively and positively? Be sure to remedy the former and accentuate the latter!

72.

"I Want to Live Here!"

You can have a house that is absolutely free of chaos and debris. It can be so organized, in fact, that it should be photographed in a magazine—and yet, the atmosphere in the home can be icy cold, and no one will be moved to make an offer. You want to do all of the little things that make your home inviting to others. As you give some thought to this, you will be able to come up with a list that's unique to you and your home.

Most people begin their day with a cup of coffee. The aroma of coffee brewing is, therefore, very enticing. Boil some water and add some coffee. Turn the heat down to a simmer. You won't have a drink you can enjoy, but you will have the fragrance of coffee filling your home for hours.

Potpourri, scented candles, and air fresheners are delightful. They may, however, instantly turn off a prospective buyer with allergies. It's best to keep any fragrance you use to just a "suggestion."

Fresh flowers on the dining room table, in the master suite, and in the bathrooms can make your home seem quite warm and beautiful. You don't have to have expensive arrangements. You can purchase flowers at the supermarket and do your own arrangements. You might want to have soft music as a background sound for a later afternoon or early evening showing of your home, as well.

Finally, it's wonderful to have signs of life in the home. For example, a whimsical bowl full of water for a dog or a cat sitting on the kitchen floor makes one smile. If you have children, you will, of course, keep their rooms tidy. Have their collections of stuffed animals arranged in a welcoming fashion on the bed or a chair. You'll make parents with children feel that their children will love this room, too.

73.

"Help" from Fido and Fluffy

In general, you'll want to keep your animals away from your prospective buyers. One never knows who might have an allergy or simply not be an "animal person." It's also less stressful for the animals, who may wonder why strangers are suddenly allowed to traipse through their home.

As with most guidelines, there are exceptions. If you are showing your current home by appointment only, you might want to ask your real estate agent to find out how the prospective buyers feel about animals. If they are dyed-in-the-wool dog fans, for instance, it might behoove you to have your well-behaved dog in the house when they come to call. The key phrase here is, of course, "well-behaved." Dog and cat people often have an instant affinity for people who share their feelings about animals. So if Fido or Fluffy helps sell your home, be sure the animal gets an extra treat!

74.

Priced to Sell

In formulating an asking price for your current home, your safest bet is to work with an experienced real estate agent who can help you establish an appropriate number. You'll want the asking price to be realistic and competitive, and you'll want to leave yourself a little wiggle room so that you can come down if you have to. In the event that you choose to work alone, here are some guidelines to help you price your home to sell.

Check the ads for homes in your neighborhood. What are people asking for homes similar to yours?

Have you done any remodeling or added amenities to the house that will enable you to legitimately raise your price above the current market? Be sure that you have your paperwork, such as receipts for all home improvement work.

Talk to your neighbors. Are there any new arrivals who might share what they paid? Do you know of any others who are contemplating a sale?

Try doing some research on the Internet. Every major real estate company has a site that will help you learn more about comparisons in your area. You can also try the major search engines. Type in "real estate sales," and a wealth of resources will be revealed.

75.

Coordinating Escrows

The term "escrow" refers to the final deposit that is delivered upon the fulfillment of terms and the exchange of the title of your home. One potential complication in any set of multiple real estate transactions is coordinating the close of escrows. For example, if you have sold your home and purchased another, and that owner has in turn purchased a new home, there are at least three escrows to coordinate. You cannot legally take possession of your new home until escrow closes.

If the buyers and sellers are on good terms, very often the length of the various escrows can be either shortened or lengthened to accommodate everyone in the transaction. Your real estate agent is your best ally in this situation.

If it happens that your escrow closing cannot be coordinated with your move from your old home, and you will be unable to move into your new home for a few days to a week, remember that your mover may have his own storage facility for your goods. Check with your tax preparer to see which, if any, additional expenses will be deductions for you.

This is a tricky situation but one that usually resolves itself amicably when professionals are handling the negotiations. You'll find that most people with whom you are doing real estate transactions share the same need for quick resolution of closing issues. If the escrows cannot be coordinated perfectly, perhaps a family member or good friend can house you for the necessary time.

76.

Clearing the Space

In many parts of the world, and indeed, in most spiritual philosophies, there are ways to "clear the space" and prepare it for new occupants. One such way is the Native American tradition of using sage. You can buy a sage stick at any store specializing in new-age products, some bookstores, most health-food stores, and even some grocery stores. A sage stick is merely a bundle of dried sage leaves.

Light the end of the sage stick with a match. You might want to do this over a sink the first time. It shouldn't be a huge pyrotechnic display. Let the flame burn for a few minutes, and then gently blow it out. Plumes of fragrant smoke will rise up. Gently blowing on the stick will revive the smoke when it begins to wane.

Now walk through each room in the house waving the stick. Ask that any negative energy left in the room from arguments, painful news, illness, and the like be banished. Trace the outline of the doors and windows. Ask that only those who truly love and support the members of this family enter this home.

If you wish to be thorough, you can include the garage, the porches, and even the front and backyards. Be sure to extinguish the embers. You can actually leave the stick in a small vase in a room like the kitchen or the bathroom. It will burn itself out shortly, and the room will be graced with the added fragrance.

It would be a nice gesture to perform this simple ceremony as you leave your old residence. This will cleanse the space of your energies and allow the new family to write its own history in the space. This ceremony can be shared with your entire family the first time as a way to unite everyone in the new surroundings. Many people, by the way, perform this ritual every week to keep the good energy strong. You'll have to make that decision after your first experience.

77.

Cleaning the New Home

Moving is a very big task and one that will tire even the most organized person. Give yourself a break, and have someone else clean the new home before you arrive. If you are moving to a new city, ask your real estate agent, a family member, or a friend to recommend a cleaning person or service who can prepare the home for your arrival. You don't want to have to deal with the previous owner's dirt the first night in your new home.

You can put down plastic sheeting and mover's pads to create walkways on move-in day. Ask everyone involved to be mindful of the clean environment. Ask them, for example, not to put their hands on walls and doors. Some people unconsciously tend to hold themselves up by leaning against a wall or holding onto a door. They don't realize that they are leaving fingerprints behind. Most of all, direct everyone to the designated bathroom. The environment will have some debris due to the chaos of the day, but it will be easy to tidy up.

By the way, if you want shelves lined with Con-Tact paper, ask the service if they perform this task. You'll be able to unpack the kitchen immediately. If not, bring your drawer liner and Con-Tact paper with you, and enlist the help of one of your friends. You may not want others to unpack your boxes and put things away. Anyone, however, can put down paper.

If your cleaning person or service does windows, be sure to have them cleaned, as well. Starting over can be difficult. Walking into a clean environment may just make the transition a bit easier.

Ask your cleaning person or service to return in about a week for another cleaning when most of the boxes are gone. This time, the cleaners will be tidying up after you rather than the previous owners.

78.

Stocking the Kitchen

O ne of the first things that you'll want to do is to stock your pantry and refrigerator. Nothing makes a new house feel like home more quickly than finding your favorite foods on hand. This will be especially important to children and teens. Long before you move, you can begin working on a master list of household foods and cleaning supplies. Creating such a list takes only a few minutes if you have a computer. Make categories for yourself, and fill in the blanks. Place a box to check off next to each item once you have it in the house. Keep a copy on the refrigerator at all times, and invite every family member to inform you when they see things running low. Your list might start with something like this.

Cleaning Supplies
- Cleanser
- Soap
- Detergent

- Glass cleaner
- Sponges
- Silver polish

Food
- Pasta
- Sauces
- Fruit
- Vegetables
- Rice
- Beans
- Tuna
- Chicken
- Soups

Family members are used to having condiments, frozen meals, butter, eggs, and the like at their immediate disposal. It may seem odd to you to think of food as one of the key ingredients in turning a house into a home. Remember, it's no accident that food is called a source of comfort.

79.

Scheduling Repairs and Construction

When you rent a home, you are less likely to make any expensive improvements. If you spot some minor changes or additions that you'd like to make (for example, to add an extra shelf in a closet or put a folding door across the washer and dryer), try to schedule a handyman to come in and finish the work before you move in. If this isn't possible, schedule this work while you are getting settled. The most careful carpenter in the world is going to create some mess. Try to get this out of the way so that your initial cleaning will truly be preparing the house for your family.

If you want to redo a closet, don't unpack your clothes until that work is completed. You'll wind up with sawdust on your clothes, or else you'll have to pile them on your bed while the work is done. Before you put them back, you may have to wash or send most to the cleaners.

If you are purchasing your home, make a list of what you feel needs to be done. Prioritize the list, and schedule the work over time, if necessary, to save your budget. If you are going to be doing extensive remodeling in a critical part of the house (the kitchen or a bathroom), you may want to delay moving in until the work is completed. Your mover will no doubt have a storage facility where your goods will be secure.

80.

What You Have Versus What You Want

Very often, the new house, condo, or apartment that we choose has aspects that appeal to the lifestyle that we want to create. Perhaps we long to entertain more and now have a spacious dining room. What if you have been living in an apartment and suddenly have a large backyard and swimming pool? Your desire to become a barbecue king or queen may surface. There are endless scenarios for how our lives are changed by our physical space.

These changes sometimes have an unusual side effect: Our current furniture, decorative items, and rugs really don't work well in the new environment. An ultra-modern condo in a beachside community in California would have furnishings that would look out of place in a brownstone in Manhattan. Very few people have the means to totally divest themselves of their current possessions and start over.

When you are working on your floor plan before the move, be sure that you place your belongings not only where they will physically fit, but also where they will look best in the new environment. You may find that, using these criteria, a lot of your furnishings should be stored, given away, or sold. This could be an excellent way to raise additional decorating funds.

After you are unpacked and settled in, why not make your need to redecorate into a game that you can enjoy? Tell family and friends that you are in no rush and have a plan of attack that will make the house perfect in whatever time period is comfortable for you. Spend time going to flea markets, antiques shops, and sales. Collect a lot of pictures of interiors that you like from magazines. Begin to isolate from these photos the elements that you'd like to duplicate. Over time, this will help you better identify what makes you unique and how to express it in your new environment.

81.

Prioritizing Your Decorating Wish List

If your new home contains a bonus area like a pool cabana or an extra bedroom for guests, creating a decorating wish list is an easy task. You need to purchase only what these new areas require in the way of furnishings. Do you have an extra bedroom set? Perhaps all you will need here are new linens and lamps. Did you have a grill in your old home? Perhaps you can make do with that, but a picnic table and chairs are in order. The other factor that you need to consider after your wish list of purchases has been created is how quickly you can afford them without breaking the bank.

A greater challenge arises when just about every area of the new home cries out for a change of decoration. As with your move, you'll best be served by crafting a plan. This will give you control, especially when it comes to impulse spending. Here are a few steps to creating your decorating priorities.

Make a list of every room in the home. For each, write down the items that you feel the room needs.

Decide which items are fairly mandatory and which are the ones that fall into the "finishing touches" category. Again, do this for every room.

Choose whether you want to work room-by-room, completing an entire room before you move to the next, or if you would be happiest purchasing big-ticket items and filling in the details over time.

Finally, prioritize your list. What is the room order you will follow to work through the house?

Doing this takes some time and thought. It's better to have a plan when faced with a large undertaking like decorating a new space. Isn't it safe to say at this point that having a plan for your move proved invaluable?

82.

Establish a Decorating Budget

Numbers don't lie, so the best way to establish a realistic decorating budget is to "run the numbers." Sit down with pen and paper, and ask yourself a series of practical, money-related questions. Does this home require more in monthly maintenance than your last? Are you the sole breadwinner in the home? Was this move inspired by a new job and a hefty pay increase? How much money will be left after you factor in the increased or decreased monthly expenditures? If you are married, are you both employed? Put your personal situation down in dollars and cents. When you have considered all of the factors, how much money is left for you to allocate to decorating?

Once you have your figure and know which room is the first to be tackled, check your list of necessary purchases and projects for the room. How much will each item cost? Is there any way to save some money? Could you, for example, do any of the repair work yourself? Are you good at painting or wallpapering? Is there someone in your family who could perform one of these tasks for a much lower rate than a professional? Make a plan of attack. If you work wisely, you might wind up with some extra money that you can put into the next room to be decorated!

83.

Working with a Decorator

Seeking a professional decorator to help you put your decorating stamp on your home can actually save you money. Professional decorators have contacts in many areas of home design and can negotiate for rates that you might not be able to secure. They have faced decorating challenges like yours countless times and can offer solutions that you might never consider. A decorator, by the way, doesn't have to do your entire home. If you feel confident about completing the master suite, for example, but are clueless as to how to tackle the living room, your decorator can concentrate on that one area.

If you have no idea what style best reflects your personal taste, take some time to study fashion and decorating magazines. Gather some photos that you relate to emotionally. Don't judge what you are saving. Simply tear out what you like. After a few weeks, you will begin to see clues. Your love of bold colors, intricate patterns, whimsical art, or traditional furniture will reveal itself. Once you identify your style, interview several decorators known for their work in this area. You might also consider interviewing professionals who may not exactly match your style, but who come with recommendations from friends. Interior designers are professionals who can adapt their own preferences to allow for a client's personal taste. Designers who may not share your exact tastes will still be able to steer you in a direction that you will be both proud of and satisfied with. As with all professionals, a personal reference is best, so keep your eyes, ears, and options open.

84.

Documenting the Changes

Odds are that if you just purchased a new home, it will be yours for years to come. Many people enjoy documenting the changes in a home that they are remodeling and/or redecorating. It really is not only a wonderful record of all of your hard work, it's a great tool to have when the time comes to sell your home. You can show interested buyers how you upgraded the property.

There is no right or wrong way to go about creating your record. You can take traditional photographs over time and put them in a photo album with your notes underneath each photo. Be sure to add the date. You can also take digital photos and create an online album for those family and friends that you left behind. This project can be a wonderful tool for staying in touch!

In years to come, visitors who admire your album may want to know how much you spent on various phases of your project. You can keep a log in the back of the album if you are open to sharing this information. The receipts themselves should be kept together in your business files.

85.

Does the Outside Reflect You?

Landscaping won't be the first thing that you do in your new home, but it shouldn't be the last, either. Your home is, in fact, the entire piece of property, not just the four walls of your house. Every aspect of it should reflect you and your family. Give some thought to what you'd like to convey to passersby. Remember to set up your outside areas for enjoyment in all seasons.

Do you want any decorative items on your lawn? These can be items that you purchase, or you can have shrubs cut into interesting shapes.

Do you enjoy cooking outside? Can you establish a place for an outdoor grill? Do you want to have a table and chairs? Will they be seasonal, or wood that's treated to stand up to winter?

Do you have a pool? Is it fenced in to protect young children and animals from drowning? Do you have seasonal toys for the pool? Do you have umbrellas to provide shade on sunny days?

Are you a container gardener? Have you decided what to plant and where to place the pots?

Will you need a professional gardener or will you be maintaining the lawn? Do you need to purchase equipment like a lawn mower, leaf blower, or small snow plow?

Are you used to gardening in a different climate? For example, have you moved from a temperate zone to an area with four full seasons? Are you going to take some classes at the local nursery?

The outside of your home is truly an extension of the world that you create within the four walls inside. Don't let the outside be neglected or underused. Not everyone has the gift of property. Be sure that you enjoy yours!

86.

Unpacking: House to Home

Just as you had a strategy and a plan to get out of your old home, you'll want to have a game plan to settle in the new one. What, for example, are the most important areas to you? These should be unpacked and settled as soon as possible. For most people, the kitchen, bathroom, and bedrooms take precedence. We need to eat and sleep in peace.

Do you need outside vendors to help settle your home? If so, make a list and schedule them. A typical move will have all or some of the following cast of characters coming to the house.

- Housecleaning crew
- Window washers
- Appliance maintenance or setup crew
- Entertainment setup crew
- Professional picture hangers
- Alarm system installation crew
- Gardener

One of the key ingredients in getting settled is removing all traces of the move. This means that boxes should be broken down, stacked, and tied for removal. Packing paper should be checked and then stuffed into garbage bags as soon as possible. You're home when those elements have been eliminated and pictures are hanging on the walls.

87.

Organizing This Home

If you spend a good deal of your time reading magazines and watching home and garden shows on TV, savoring ideas for how you want your home to be, take note. Moving is perhaps the best opportunity that you'll ever have to lay the foundation for an organized home. The most beautifully decorated home in the world is going to look shabby if it's encrusted with piles of newspapers, old magazines, and untended mail. If toiletries hog the bathroom counter and clothes are draped on every surface in the bedroom, no decoration will save this home from looking unkempt.

If you have just purchased a home or condo, see if the closets are adequate for your clothes. If not, consider having a professional closet company come out and add some shelves and extra rods. You'll be able to have an organized closet from day one.

Every unorganized human has a super-organized friend or family member. Ask this person to help you weed out the bathroom toiletries that you do not need. Then have them take you shopping for the containers that will simplify your life in the new space.

Do you have a collection that is out of hand? Take some time to research the ways other people organize these items. You may not get it done before you move, but you'll know what supplies you need at the new house. For example, a cottage industry has grown around the safe and decorative ways to store photos and make albums. What are you waiting for?

88.

What Is a Professional Organizer?

If suggestions on how to organize your home fill you with dread instead of anticipation, help is at hand. You may need the services of a professional organizer.

A professional organizer is a consultant who restores order where there is chaos. Professional organizers traditionally have specialties. For example, you can find some who only create office systems. Others will specialize in time management. Still others will have home specialties like closet and kitchen organization. Of course, there are those who make a career out of helping others move.

If the very idea of moving has you overwhelmed, you might want to hire a professional organizer to assist you. She or he can help from the very beginning and basically take over the entire process, including unpacking you in your new home. Alternately, he or she can be asked to assist with one phase of the move. For example, you might want your organizer to supervise the moving crew on pack-up and move-in day, because it is too emotional for you; or while you are supervising the movers at the new home, your professional organizer can be unpacking the clothes closets and emergency kits. Whatever your needs, a professional organizer with a specialty in moving can make this process a little easier.

89.

Locating a Professional Organizer

Like all professional consultants that you would hire, from your mover to your plumber, the best are found through personal referral. Begin your search by asking family and friends if they or anyone they know has had a positive experience with a professional organizer. Don't be shy about asking up to three organizers to come to your home and meet with you. Like your mover, this person is going to be involved in the intimate details of your life. You want someone who is not only skilled at what he or she does, but who is a perfect fit with you personality-wise.

If you come up dry in this search, there are other ways to find your organizer. Look in your local phone book. Ask your real estate agent if he or she can recommend anyone. See if the local newspaper or the chamber of commerce has any leads. If all else fails, contact the National Association of Professional Organizers (NAPO), and they will have referrals by specialty. Their web address is http://www.napo.net/. You can also reach them by phone at (770) 325-3440. Just as it sounds, this is a national organization boasting a membership of well over a thousand members devoted to supporting the profession.

We all have a limited amount of energy to expend. You might want to weigh the value of having someone else do the grunt work of your move so that you can dedicate yourself to the care of your family and perhaps the new job that you're excited about. A professional organizer is the ideal solution—especially one who specializes in moving. He or she will, in fact, probably have a host of professionals from movers to plumbers to refer to you.

90.

What's Feng Shui All About?

*F*eng Shui is an ancient Chinese practice. It is referred to in many circles as "the art of placement." The Chinese believe that everything is made of energy, or *chi*. When you build a house, you enclose chi in one area. Using an eight-sided diagram called the *bagua*, you can enter the home and find all of the major areas of life governed by specific areas of the home.

The easiest example to look at is the entry of the home. This corresponds to the entry point of the bagua. The color used here is black. The element is water. In most Chinese restaurants, you have probably noted a large fish tank near the front door. The water represents money flowing into the home or business from one's career. Water that is moving is even better symbolically, as you can imagine. Hence the fish and the pump! Note that fish tanks are black.

The areas of life found on the bagua and in your home with their colors and elements are:

- Career/black/water
- Skill and knowledge/blue
- Family and wealth/green/wood
- Prosperity/purple
- Fame and reputation/red/fire
- Relationships/pink
- Creativity/white/silver
- Helpfulness/gray
- Health (center of the bagua)/yellow

These follow the bagua, working in a clockwise direction from the doorway. In the center of the bagua is health. You would designate an area of your home to govern health. In fact, there would be an area of each room and of the house as a whole that governs each of these life areas.

In the end, Feng Shui is simply another way for you to bless your home and its occupants. If Feng Shui intrigues you, there is a wonderful assortment of books in the marketplace that will deepen your knowledge. Should you wish to read more about this fascinating art, be aware that there are two major schools of Feng Shui: the traditional Chinese compass school and the Black Hat or Intuitive School. The latter incorporates many elements from Tibetan Buddhism.

91.

Basic Feng Shui Supplies

Each system of Feng Shui will have supplies unique to the tenets governing the practice. The supplies listed here are in accordance with the Black Hat tradition. They form a rudimentary start for the novice. Some may have to be purchased, while others can surely be found in your home.

- Water fountain
- Bamboo flutes
- Chimes
- Candles
- Elephants (not the real kind)
- Bagua mirrors (found in arts and crafts stores)

You will probably want at least one water fountain in your home. It can be beneficial to your career if placed just inside the front door to the home or just inside the door to the home office. Remember that black is the color and metal represents water. A black wrought-iron stand for your fountain will really make your desire for good fortune in your career a lot stronger.

Most people are concerned about relationships. We either want one or we'd like to improve the one that we have. The far right corner of any room as seen from the main entrance is the area governing relationships in Feng Shui. You'll want everything in twos here. Pictures of happily married couples work well. That painting of your old maid Aunt Sarah isn't the thing for your relationship corner, if you're looking for a partner. The color is pink, but you don't have to have the colors of the bagua visible. You can trace a bagua in pink construction paper, for example, and place it behind a picture in this corner or tape it under a table. You can also hide baguas under furniture cushions. Bagua mirrors can be placed at entrances to boost career energy. Let your imagination be your guide.

As you can see, there are ancient traditions in Feng Shui, but there is also room for your personal creativity. This practice is serious, but you are certainly welcome to enjoy the process—not to mention the results.

92.

Removing the Debris from Moving Day

As you unpack your home, it's best to have someone who comes every few hours just to break down the boxes and check the wrapping paper for missed possessions. This will enable you to move more quickly from several perspectives. First of all, you will know that you haven't accidentally tossed away some tiny, critical possession. What is a sugar bowl without its spoon? Secondly, you will need space to work. As empty boxes pile up around you, it's critical to have your work area restored.

Let's say that you are working in the dining room, and after unpacking a few lampshades, you now unpack the good china. You not only have an even bigger box in the area, you have a mound of paper.

Finally, it's a psychological boost to see that stack of empty, flat boxes get higher and higher. It's a clear indicator of the progress that you are making. A stack of unpacked boxes still taped together will ultimately dwarf you physically and drain your energy. Such stacks end up in the corners of a room, taking up needed space and contributing to the general disarray of the day. A stack of boxes ready for refuse pickup will inspire you to continue working. Get these boxes out of your house and either into the garage or by the curb for refuse removal.

If you are unable to have someone help who is solely devoted to the task of box removal, then it might be a good idea to break down your boxes as you go along. Unpack, break down, and stack. Every hour or so, take a break from unpacking and remove the debris. Unpacking a home is hard, physical work. You want to give yourself every edge.

93.

Does It All Get Unpacked?

In a word, yes, it does. Leaving things in boxes makes a statement. It says that you haven't taken ownership of the new space. Perhaps you were forced to make this move due to circumstances beyond your control. Perhaps you were asked to choose a location that suited other family members. Perhaps you are not feeling completely well and have the flu. No matter how resistant we are to change, once it has become a reality, our greatest success comes when we fully embrace the new circumstances. In the world of moving, to fully embrace the experience, we need to free our beloved possessions from the limbo of boxes.

Some boxes that traditionally get left, sometimes for weeks on end, are those containing the pictures, artwork, and mirrors that adorn our walls. These boxes are very narrow and don't take up a lot of room. We postpone painting or laying new carpet and tell ourselves that when those things are done, we will hang things on the walls. Ironically, this gives our home an unfinished, sterile look much like a prison or a hospital.

You may, of course, have a legitimate reason for leaving some boxes in tidy stacks in the garage. Perhaps this move is temporary and there would be no point in unpacking ten boxes of books. Perhaps you have moved from the Snow Belt to the Sun Belt and have decided to keep all of your ski clothes and equipment packed till next season. There isn't any reason to feel guilty if you have made such a decision. Just remember that the day your last box is unpacked, you'll know that your commitment to this move, this new home, and the new life that it represents is complete. The time frame for that moment is personal.

94.

Can You Drive into the Garage?

The garage more often than not becomes a secret zone for the chaos that we keep hidden from family and friends. The home looks perfect. The cars, however, need to live on the street because our world of unmade decisions is sitting in the garage in boxes and in piles. If you live in the Sun Belt, where the temperatures are generally temperate, your car will not suffer. The colder climes are another story for your vehicle.

Think of your garage as another room in your home. You wouldn't accept a living room that looked like a war zone, so why accept a garage that does? Here is a world where your teenagers can assist you in getting organized. They and perhaps a few friends can haul and place the heavy tools, camping equipment, sports paraphernalia, gardening equipment, and the like that may be too heavy for you. They probably won't be interested in picking the drapes for the new living room, but choosing the best workbench for the garage may be right up their alley.

A wall of built-in cabinets is ideal for the garage. You can also buy some heavy-duty shelving units at your local home store if you don't want to make a huge investment or are renting the home. The important thing is to get items off the ground and out of piles so that the family car can have some floor space.

If you're thinking that this is all very unimportant to you, consider this: The garage is probably the last part of your home that you see when you leave and the first view that greets you when you return home. If it's in chaos, it will be a constant reminder of unfinished business.

95.

Establishing Roots

If you weren't able to get all of the suggested neighborhood information before you moved, once the truck leaves your driveway, a family member should be put in charge of obtaining this information. Older children and teens, who weren't necessarily thrilled about making this change, can be put in charge of information-gathering. This is a great way to ease them into their new lives.

If you obtained the information but did not have a chance to act on it, be sure to make time to visit and choose your new church or synagogue. Check out the local gym and nail salon. Whatever activities made up your routine in the old neighborhood should be duplicated in the new one. It's the little things that tell us that we are home—for instance, knowing where to have your hair cut when the time comes or having a craving for Italian food and knowing which restaurant to call for reservations.

If you sit in a perfectly organized home, with every last box unpacked and every room a decorator's delight, but you never venture out to put down roots, guess what? You haven't made a commitment to your new life. Embracing your neighbors, the neighborhood, and the city that you now call home will be the final elements of the move you started on the day you packed the first box.

96.

Adjusting to a New School

There are two key ways to help your children make a successful transition to a new school. The first involves becoming actively involved in the school. Do they need parent volunteers in the classroom? Is there a PTA you could join? Is a school dance on the horizon looking for chaperones? Can you join a committee and offer to do some projects at home? Getting involved in your kids' world is a wonderful way to show that you care.

The second thing you can do is to become active in the community itself. If you want your children to adjust to their new surroundings, you can model the behavior that you hope to see in them. If you work full time, and your ability to volunteer at their school is minimal, you can talk openly at meal times about your experience as "the new kid on the business block."

We're all afraid of the unknown, and very few people jump with total abandon into a new experience. If your children hear that you have anxious moments, they will be comforted. If you started the tradition of family meetings before your move, there is no reason not to continue them now. Communication about every aspect of this new life will strengthen the family bond and those fledgling roots that you've planted in the community.

97.

Joining a Synagogue or Church

The person with current ties to a house of worship will usually find a new spiritual home as soon as he or she makes a move. If you haven't been active at a church or synagogue since childhood, a move is a wonderful time to consider reestablishing those ties. In addition to sustenance for your soul, you'll open yourself to a host of practical advantages. Are you looking for like-minded individuals who might become friends? Do you need to find reliable baby-sitters with good recommendations? Do you wish that you could ask some natives where the best restaurants are located? Your house of worship can fill all of these needs.

In large cities, there are churches and synagogues with huge congregations. Here, in addition to the above, you can find stimulating lecture series, twelve-step meetings, and even travel programs. If you are shy and moving to a new city is especially difficult for you, remember that support on many levels is waiting for you at your local house of worship. You can make investigating the various places to worship part of the great adventure that this move represents.

Joining a house of worship can offer a sense of community and closeness that is unique. It is comforting to realize that there is always a place where you can belong. It is important to be able to find a sense of peace amidst the chaos and change of life. In a new community, a house of worship is just the place to find your oasis of calm.

98.

Keeping Track of the Paperwork

There are two basic ways to keep the myriad number of phone numbers, addresses, contacts, and receipts for your move in an organized fashion: Use a large ring binder with tabs for your various categories, or use a file box or file cabinet drawer. If you are computer savvy and prefer to work this way, you'll want to print out hard copies of all of your information or keep it on a disc. Computers crash, and you don't want to lose everything that you researched over the last weeks or months.

You need to be able to put your hands on items at a moment's notice. Whatever system you choose (even one of your own design), that's the bottom line that needs to be served. When the move is behind you, and you are completely unpacked and settled in, you may want to go through this material before you decide to save it all forever. Some things you simply won't need anymore, and they can be tossed. For example, if you interviewed three movers, the only information that you may need to access anymore will be about the mover you hired.

After the move, all of the brochures on moving and packing that these companies gave you can also be eliminated from your files. In much the same way, every facility and vendor that you investigated, from schools and churches to plumbers and architects, can be tossed if you didn't decide to use their services.

On the other hand, you'll want to keep some information for its long-term value. For example, keep those tax-deductible receipts handy for the person who prepares your return. The appliances that you purchased all come with warranties and instructions. You can attach your purchase receipts and store these with all household and office warranties in your file cabinet.

In preparing for this move, you divested yourself of many items that you no longer needed in your life. Once you arrive at the new home, make the process of weeding out a permanent part of how you live. The next time you move, there may not be any weeding and tossing. You can simply tell the movers to pack whatever they see. After all, if they see it, you want it!

99.

An Attitude of Gratitude

Nothing in life is perfect. Your move will be no exception. Something is bound to get lost or broken, even with the most careful movers and friends on board to assist you. Things will take longer than you imagined. Phone numbers will be misplaced. Vendors may prove to be flaky. The list of possibilities is endless.

These snafus, whether major or minor, obviously need to be handled. The key is to deal with each situation and move on. Human beings frequently hold on to negative experiences. We retell the story of the clumsy mover or the incompetent plumber, all the while not realizing that this repetition feeds the fires of emotional upset.

Why not make a concerted effort to retell the positive stories that came out of this move? Who went out of their way to assist you? Who among your friends rallied to your side? Which new vendors turned out to be artists at what they do for a living? We all have these experiences, along with the negative, disappointing moments of life. Which will you choose to feed?

In the final analysis, you are at last in your new location. Whether you moved into a studio apartment or a mansion, be grateful for the roof over your head and the loved ones who share the space. Being grateful will fill your heart with joy and expectation of good. You know the old phrase: Like attracts like. New friends, new experiences, and many new surprises await you. All you have to do is open yourself to receiving them.

100.

Take Stock

The first four to six weeks in your new location often go by in a blur. You are overwhelmed with unpacking, finding your way throughout your community, settling your children into their new routines, and finding a place for yourself to fit in. It isn't often during this initial time period that you stop to take stock—to evaluate how far you and your family have come in this short time, and what still needs to be attended to.

This is exactly the right time to call a family meeting. Set aside some quiet time to discuss where your family is on the adjustment scale. Your children will surely want to express either their excitement or dissatisfaction with their new surroundings. Giving them an open forum to report both the positive and negative aspects of their new lives can be liberating for them. Let them know that you don't expect them to behave as if everything is perfect—you really want to hear their honest reactions to what has been thrust upon them. You may find that your children are thriving, or you may find that they need some extra help and attention from you in some areas where they are struggling.

Is your spouse handling the move well? Perhaps he or she has taken on a more demanding job and isn't around as much. How does that make the family feel? Maybe you or your spouse don't feel that you are making inroads in the community because you are busy taking care of setting up house and home. Is anyone homesick for old friends, school, or family left behind?

You can discuss these issues, and as a family, decide what can be done about them. If your spouse is feeling overworked and disconnected from your new surroundings, suggest having an informal neighborhood get-together so that he or she can meet people one on one. If your children are having trouble making friends, perhaps enrolling them in some extracurricular sports or classes will help them find kids to relate to. By taking stock of how everyone in the family is feeling, no one feels left out or unattended to.

You made this move as a family, and it should be tackled as such. Keeping the lines of communication open amidst the whirlwind of moving in and getting settled is important. You and your family will be happier if you put the details of daily life aside for an evening and concentrate on the larger issues that will ultimately bring happiness to everyone.